DATE DUE	
JUL 2 4 '91		
MAR 1 9 2002		
APR 0 9 2002		

WHAT IS INTELLIGENCE?

What Is Intelligence?

Contemporary Viewpoints on Its Nature and Definition

Editors

Robert J. Sternberg

Yale University

Douglas K. Detterman

Case Western Reserve University

ABLEX PUBLISHING CORPORATION
NORWOOD, NEW JERSEY

Copyright © 1986 by Ablex Publishing Corporation
Second Printing 1988.

Library of Congress Cataloging-in-Publication Data

Main entry under title:

What is intelligence?

    Bibliography: p.
    Includes indexes.

I. Sternberg, Robert J. II. Detterman, Douglas K.

ISBN 0-89391-373-1
ISBN 0-89391-389-8 (pbk.)

Ablex Publishing Corporation
355 Chestnut Street
Norwood, New Jersey 07648

Contents

Part III.   Integrations

Preface

Few psychological phenomena are as elusive as intelligence. Indeed, psychologists cannot even quite agree as to just what intelligence is. Yet there are few psychological phenomena of greater interest and importance both to science and to society, and psychologists have been busy studying the construct for decades. Today we seem a long way off from understanding the nature of intelligence. But have we made any progress in recent years or decades, or are we still basically where we were when we started? The brief essays in this book provide us with a data base for answering this question.

Sixty-five years ago, a classic symposium was published in the *Journal of Educational Psychology*. The symposium, convened by the editors of the journal, was entitled "Intelligence and Its Measurement," and it brought together many of the most prominent psychological theorists in the area of intelligence research to address two issues:

"(1) What I conceive 'intelligence' to be, and by what means it can best be measured by group tests. (For example, should the material call into play analytical and higher thought processes? Or, should it deal equally or more considerably with simple, associative, and perceptual processes, etc.?)

"(2) What are the most crucial 'next steps' in research?"

Although six and a half decades have passed since the publication of this significant and widely cited symposium, the effort has not been repeated. The present book seeks to update the symposium, addressing these issues in a way that reflects progress that has been made from the beginning to the ending years of the twentieth century. What do theorists of intelligence today believe intelligence to be? How can it best be measured? What are the next steps in research? How have contemporary views changed from previous ones? The present book is intended to address, and possibly to answer, each of these questions.

This book represents a collection of two dozen brief essays by foremost experts in the field of intelligence, who were asked to respond to the very same questions that were posed to the experts in the 1921 symposium. Each expert was asked to write briefly on the topics of the nature of intelligence, its measurement, and the future of research in the field, bringing his or her own perspective to bear on the issues. Happily, almost all of the experts contacted agreed to participate in the project. We present here the essays, and integrative material to help interrelate these contemporary essays, as well as to interrelate these essays to those of the earlier symposium. We believe that the present set of essays shows the progress that has been made toward understanding the nature and measurement of intelligence. We hope that this volume, like the previous one, will exert a constructive influence in helping to define an elusive construct for an elusive field—that of intelligence.

RJS
DKD

PART I

INTRODUCTION

1.

A Framework for Understanding Conceptions of Intelligence

Robert J. Sternberg

Yale University

This book presents two dozen definitions of intelligence. Although extraordinary diversity can be found within these definitions, there are striking commonalities as well. In this introduction, I shall try to do justice to both the similarities and the differences among the definitions by summarizing what the definitions are, and placing them into an integrative framework. First, I shall present the framework, and then show how it applies to each individual definition in this volume.

The Framework

The proposed framework for understanding conceptions of intelligence is shown in Table 1.

The theorists in this volume identify three main loci of intelligence—intelligence within the individual, intelligence within the environment, and intelligence within the interaction between the individual and the environment. Within these three main loci, however, there are a number of more specific loci for intelligence.

Theorists identifying intelligence as within the individual seem to be dealing with three main levels of analysis: a biological level, a molar level, and a behavioral level.

The biological level can be established either across or within organisms. Consider in turn each of these viewpoints.

Table 1.   Loci of Intelligence

I. In Individual
   A. Biological Level
      1. Across Organisms
         a. Between Species (evolution)
         b. Within Species (genetics)
         c. Between-Within Interaction
      2. Within Organisms
         a. Structure
         b. Process
         c. Structure-Process Interaction
      3. Across-Within Interaction
   B. Molar Level
      1. Cognitive
         a. Metacognition
            i. Processes
            ii. Knowledge
            iii. Process-Knowledge Interaction
         b. Cognition
            i. Processes
               (a) selective attention
               (b) learning
               (c) reasoning
               (d) problem solving
               (e) decision making
            ii. Knowledge
            iii. Process-Knowledge Interaction
         c. Metacognition-Cognition Interaction
      2. Motivational
         a. Level (Magnitude) of Energy
         b. Direction (Disposition) of Energy
         c. Level-Direction Interaction
   C. Behavioral Level
      1. Academic
         a. Domain-General
         b. Domain-Specific
         c. General-Specific Interaction
      2. Social
         a. Within-Person
         b. Between-Persons
         c. Within-Between Interaction
      3. Practical
         a. Occupational
         b. Everyday Living
         c. Occupational–Everyday Living Interaction
   D. Biological-Molar-Behavioral Interaction
II. In Environment
   A. Level of Culture/Society

(*continued*)

Table 1. Loci of Intelligence (*continued*)

	1. Demands
	2. Values
	3. Demands-Values Interaction
B.	Level of Niche Within Culture/Society
	1. Demands
	2. Values
	3. Demands-Values Interaction
C.	Level × Sublevel Interaction
III.	Individual-Environment Interaction

Across organisms, one can view intelligence within the context of the evolution of species, within the context of the genetics of a single species, or within the interaction between interspecies evolution and intraspecies genetics. For example, one might consider how insects differ from rats in their intelligence, and how rats differ from humans. Or one might consider variability within any one of these species—say, humans—from one generation to the next. Or one might consider genetic transmission in both its constancies and its variabilities across generations of different species.

Within organisms, one can view intelligence in terms of structural aspects of the organism (e.g., hemispheres of the brain), or in terms of process aspects (e.g., the neuronal processes that give rise to evoked potentials). Furthermore, it is possible to look at the interaction between structure and process, considering, for example, how certain regions of the brain generate particular evoked potentials.

An integrated biological viewpoint would take into account the interaction of biological factors across and within organisms. For example, one might seek to understand the evolution of the brain and its aspects, or the genetic bases for brain development. An integrated biological approach to intelligence appears to be the ultimate goal of biologically oriented theorists.

The molar level of theorizing seems to emphasize two principal aspects of mental functioning: the cognitive and the motivational.

Cognitive theorists of intelligence deal with two main kinds of cognition—metacognition and ordinary cognition—although not all of these theorists would accept this distinction between the two kinds of cognition. Metacognition refers to knowledge about and control of one's cognition. Ordinary cognition refers to what is known and controlled by metacognition. Note that both metacognition and cognition can be divided into process and knowledge aspects. An example of metacognition as knowledge would be the awareness of what one does and does not know, whereas cognition as knowledge would be the knowledge itself. An example of metacognition as control processes would be the formation of a strategy to solve a problem, whereas an example of cognition as controlled processes would be the mental steps that are actually used to solve the problem. The processes of cognition are manifold. Theorists of intelligence seem especially to emphasize sets of processes involved in selective attention, learning, reasoning, problem solving, and decision making. Processes and knowledge interact, of course, and this interaction takes place through learning, which requires processes that bring old knowledge to bear on new knowledge. It is important to add that just as processes and knowledge interact, so do metacognition and cognition: In order to function intelligently, one must change one's metacognition to accommodate one's cognition, and vice versa. As one learns new things, for example, one must take account of this new learning in one's understanding of what one can do. For another example, when one sets up a strategy for solving a problem, one must then choose just the cognitive processes that will make the strategy a success. Whether or not one accepts the distinction proposed here and elsewhere between metacognition and ordinary cognition, both aspects of functioning would seem to be needed, regardless of what they are called or how they are classified.

Motivational theorists of intelligence argue that there is more to intelligence than cognition—that one should look to motivation as well. Indeed, much cognition is motivated (some might argue that it all is), and one's motivation to cognize may determine both the quality and the quantity of cognition. Motivational theorists focus on two principal properties of motivation—the level or magnitude of the motivation, and its direction or disposition. For example, there is, within a given individual, a motivation to learn. But this motivation is not equally directed to all kinds of learning, and hence it is necessary to take direction into account. One's intelligence is affected not only by the amount of learning that takes place, but also by the kinds of learning that take place, and both amount and kind are affected, in turn, by motivation. Level and direction of motivation interact with each other, of course, in that one may have high motivational levels in some directions, but low ones in others.

The behavioral level of analysis looks not "inside" the head, but outside it—at what the person does rather than at what he or she thinks. The argument of the behavioral theorists (who need not be behaviorists!) is that intelligence resides in one's behavior rather than in (or in addition to) the mental functioning that leads to this behavior. The behaviorally oriented theorists seem to concentrate on three main domains of behavior—academic, social, and practical.

The academic domain includes the behavior exhibited in schoolwork, including subjects such as language, mathematics, natural science, social science, and the arts. Two major controversies in theorizing about behavior need to be considered. The first concerns the breadth of behavior that falls within the domain of intelligence—for example, is artistic behavior, or dancing behavior, "intelligent" in the ordinary sense, or does it fall within some other domain? The second controversy concerns the domain-specificity of intelligence—are the processes and structures underlying intelligent behavior relatively domain-general, or relatively domain-specific? For example, are the mental processes used to solve mathematics problems the same as those used to solve social-scientific problems, and if they are not the same, just how much overlap is there? Although the argument over domain-generality is not limited to academic contents, it seems to generate the greatest controversy for these kinds of contents. Most theorists would agree that there is some domain-generality as well as some domain-specificity of functioning, and would see as their goal the determination of just which mental structures and processes fall within which class.

The social domain includes the behavior exhibited in between- as well as within-person interactions. How does a person use intelligence to facilitate interactions with other people, but also, how does a person use intelligence to facilitate interaction with (or understanding of) himself or herself? Although not all theorists would distinguish within- from between-person interactions, the distinction seems to be a viable one. People know that their understanding of themselves often seems not to match their understanding of others. The two kinds of understanding may, of course, interact: Getting to know oneself better may help one understand others better, and vice versa.

The practical domain includes the behavior exhibited in one's occupation and in one's daily living. Occupational aspects might include knowing how to perform one's job effectively, how to get ahead in one's job, and how to make the most of the job one has. Everyday-living aspects might include knowing how to balance a checkbook, how to cook for oneself, and how to shop intelligently. Theorists do not agree as to just how much the everyday domain should be considered in understanding and assessing intelligence: On the one hand, some theorists would look at cooking or shopping as mundane and as uninteresting bases for theories about individual differences in intelligence; on the other hand, some theorists would argue that it is in behaviors such as these that true understanding of intelligence is to be found. Occupational and everyday behaviors are not independent, but interactive: For example, some of us find that our preoccupation with our occupations prevents us from accomplishing or even learning how to accomplish some of the things that we need to do to make a go of our lives outside our occupations.

Although theorists often think and write as though the biological, molar, and behavioral domains are independent, it is doubtful that anyone believes this. Certainly, the three work together in ways that are not yet totally understood. Our lack of understanding sometimes leads to theoretical disagreement. For example, most molar theorists would agree that molar strucures and processes are capable, ultimately, of being understood at the biological level. But they might not agree that such understanding is the most desirable at this time, or for all purposes. An analogy often used is that of the automobile: One does not best understand the malfunctions of an automobile at the level of the atoms or molecules that contribute to the parts of that automobile. But one need not rely on analogy: Many molar theorists would argue, for example, that the EEG patterns measured by biologically oriented psychologists are a function of cognitive processes, rather than the cognitive processes being a function of the EEG. Of course, basic biological processes underlie both cognitive processing and EEG—which is, after all, only a dependent variable—but theorists differ considerably in the emphasis they place on the most fruitful level of analysis at which to pursue understanding of EEG and other dependent variables used in the measurement of intelligence.

Not all theorists view intelligence as residing within the individual: Some view it as residing within the environment, either as a function of one's culture and society, or as a function of one's niche within the culture and society, or both. For example, some would argue that intelligence is wholly relativistic with respect to culture, and hence that it is impossible to understand intelligence without understanding the culture: In essence, the culture determines the very nature of intelligence and determines who has what levels of it through labeling or attributional processes. What the culture, society, or niche within culture and society deems to be intelligent will generally be a function of the demands of the environment in which people live, the values that are held by the people within that environment, and the interaction between demands and values. For example, societal functions that are in high demand but that are not easily filled may come to be valued highly.

Many theorists of intelligence would define the locus of intelligence as occurring neither wholly within the individual nor wholly within the environment, but rather within the interaction between the two: How does the individual function—mentally and/or behaviorally—within various environmental milieux? People do not think or behave intelligently within a vacuum, nor can culture or society set standards for what constitutes intelligence without reference to the functions people perform in that culture or society. Thus it may be difficult to understand intelligence fully without first considering the interaction of the person with one or more environments, and recognizing the possibility that a person may be differentially intelligent in different environments, depending upon the demands of these various environments.

In sum, I have proposed here a framework for understanding definitions of intelligence. Now consider a précis of each of the definitions proposed in this volume, and how they fit into this framework.

Application of the Framework

Consider now each of the conceptions of intelligence represented in this volume, and how each of them fits into the proposed framework.

Anastasi conceives of intelligence as a quality of behavior (I-C in Table 1). However, she emphasizes that intelligent behavior is behavior that is adaptive, representing effective ways of meeting the demands of environments as they change (III). What constitutes adaptive behavior varies across species (I-A-1-a) and with the context in which the organism lives (II), so that intelligence is a pluralistic concept.

Baltes expresses a preference for speaking not in terms of intelligence per se, but rather in terms of the specific constructs that constitute what we ordinarily think of as intelligence—constructs such as innate intellectual capacity (I-A-1-b), intellectual reserve capacity, learning capacity (I-B-1-b-i-(b)), problem-solving ability (I-B-1-b-i-(d)), and knowledge systems (I-B-1-b-ii). He believes that by building theories in terms that permit theoretical specificity and precision, we will achieve a better understanding of intelligence than if we attempt to build a macrotheory that fails to do justice to intelligence in all of its aspects.

Baron defines intelligence as the set of abilities involved in the achievement of rationally chosen goals (I-B-1-b-i-(e)), whatever these goals might happen to be. He distinguishes between two types of abilities: capacities (I-B), which are things like mental speed (I-B-1) and mental energy (I-B-2-a); and dispositions, which include, for example, the disposition to be self-critical (I-B-2-b). Baron emphasizes that in order to be considered as components of intelligence, these capacities and dispositions must be domain-general (I-C-1-a) rather than domain-specific.

Berry views intelligence as the end product of individual development in the cognitive-psychological domain (I-B-1), as distinguished from the affective or motivational domains. Berry includes sensory and perceptual functioning, but not motor, motivational, emotional, and social functioning. He believes that intelligence is adaptive for a given cultural group in permitting members of the group, as well as the group as a whole, to operate effectively in a given ecological context (II, III).

Brown and Campione, in their definition of intelligence, emphasize especially the processes and products of learning (I-B-1-b-i-(b); I-B-1-b-ii), as well as the interaction between these processes and products (I-B-1-b-iii). These authors note that their view of the relationship of learning and

knowledge to intelligence differs from earlier views, such as that of Woodrow, in terms of their emphasis not only on speed of learning, but also on
the metacognitive processes and knowledge that interact with learning
(I-B-1-a; I-B-1-c). Brown and Campione's view also differs from earlier
views, which did not prove very fruitful, in terms of their emphasis upon
learning as it operates in the everyday environment (II), as opposed to
merely in the laboratory. These authors have collected an impressive array
of data showing how their emphasis upon the metacognitive bases of learning and upon learning as it occurs in the real world results in a much more
productive approach to the understanding of the relationship between
learning and intelligence than have earlier approaches.

Butterfield emphasizes four bases of individual differences in intelligence
that emerge from the literature of cognitive psychology. Like Brown and
Campione, he emphasizes the centrality of learning in intelligence (I-B-1-b-
i-(b)). The four aspects of Butterfield's definition are that less intelligent
people have smaller and less elaborately organized knowledge bases (I-B-1-b-
ii); that they use fewer, simpler, and more passive information-processing
strategies (I-B-1-b-i); that they have less metacognitive understanding of
their own cognitive systems and of how the functioning of these systems
depends upon the environment (I-B-1-a-ii; I-B-1-a-iii); and that they use less
complete and flexible executive processes for controlling their thinking (I-
B-1-a-i). Butterfield is especially concerned with how these four aspects of
cognition interact (I-B-1-c).

Carroll argues that the domains to which intelligence is applied are
basically threefold: academic and technical (I-C-1), social (I-C-2), and practical (I-C-3). He argues that first and foremost, intelligence must be understood as a concept in the mind of a society at large, and that the exact nature
of this concept may depend upon the society (II-A). However, he concentrates in his definition upon our own society. He limits his definition to
cognitive capacities (I-B-1), purposefully excluding motivational tendencies (I-B-2) and physical capacities. He notes that a major goal of scientific
research on intelligence is to bring to us greater understanding of the
societal concept of intelligence, as it applies in both laboratory settings and
the real world. Although the greatest success of scientific research so far has
been in studying intelligence in laboratories in academic settings (I-C-1), he
notes the importance of studying intelligence in social and practical settings
as well (I-C-2, I-C-3).

Das views intelligence as the sum total of all cognitive processes
(I-B-1), including planning (I-B-1-a-i), coding of information (I-B-1-b), and
arousal of attention (I-B-1-b-i-(a)). He believes that the cognitive processes
required for planning have the highest status, or the most central role, in
intelligence (I-B-1-a-i). Das defines planning broadly, including within it the
generation of plans and strategies, selection from among available plans, and
the execution of these plans. He also includes decision making within the

purview of intelligence (I-B-1-b-i-(e)). Das believes that it is important to understand these elements of intelligence not only in isolation, but in interaction (I-B-1-c) as well.

Detterman views intelligence as a complex system composed of numerous independent cognitive processes (I-B-1). These processes contribute to the appearance of a general factor. He draws an analogy between an intelligence test score and a global rating of a university. One can evaluate the overall quality of a university, but this overall quality is a function of many interrelated elements, working singly and together. As with intelligence, the functioning of the university can be evaluated at multiple levels.

Estes suggests that the most promising path to increasing our understanding of human intelligence may be through borrowing from recent research that has been done in artificial intelligence. He suggests that three central capacities that have been isolated in artificial intelligence research are critical for human intelligence as well: the capacity to manipulate symbols (I-B-1-b-i); the capacity to evaluate the consequences of alternative choices (I-B-1-b-i-(b); I-B-1-b-i-(e)); and the capacity to search through sequences of symbols (I-B-1-b-i-(a)). Estes also notes a critical distinction between human and animal intelligence, namely, that animals seem to concentrate on learning information that is relevant to problems that they face immediately, whereas humans tend to concentrate on learning of information whose consequences may be long-term rather than merely short-term.

Eysenck clearly concentrates on the biological (I-A) rather than the molar (I-B) bases of intelligence. Indeed, he believes that a scientific understanding of intelligence requires understanding at the biological level. He views intelligence as deriving from the error-free transmission of information through the cortex (I-A-2-b). He suggests that the use of evoked potentials measured from the cortex provides a particularly apt way of assessing accuracy of transmission.

Gardner suggests the need to understand intelligence in terms of variations in types of naturally occurring cognition in the everyday environment (II), and especially to concentrate upon the cognitive contents of intelligence (I-B-1-b). He believes that there is no one intelligence, but rather multiple, independent intelligences. He further believes that our understanding of these intelligences will increase only if we move away from laboratory studies toward an understanding of the interaction of the individual with the everyday environment (III). His approach to identifying the intelligences has drawn not upon conventional intelligence tests, but upon the end states that can be attained by a variety of individuals both within and between cultures (II-A, II-B). Gardner suggests that, at least for the present, we can identify seven different intelligences: linguistic, logical-mathematical, musical, spatial, bodily-kinesthetic, interpersonal, and intrapersonal (I-B-1, I-C).

Glaser defines intelligence as proficiency (or competence) and intellectual cognitive performance (I-B-1), using the term *intellectual* to separate out from intelligence emotional cognition. Glaser distinguishes between knowledge in artifactual domains, such as most of the academic ones (I-C), and intelligence in natural domains (II). Whereas intelligence in artifactual domains is usually acquired primarily through formal schooling (I-C-1), intelligence in natural domains is usually acquired more informally and spontaneously through interactions with the everyday world (III). Glaser develops his notion of cognitive proficiency as a basis for intelligence through an analogy to athletic proficiency.

Goodnow views intelligence as a judgment or attribution, comparable to the judgments we make about people being physically attractive or friendly, rather than as a quality residing in the individual (III). In order to understand intelligence, therefore, we should not look to intelligence tests, cognitive tasks, or physiologically based measures, but rather to the attributions people make about themselves and each other with respect to intelligence. Goodnow is explicit in emphasizing that intelligence should be viewed as encompassing situations in which people interact with one another or solve problems together (I-C-2), not merely situations in which people work on their own or interact with objects or abstract concepts. She notes that conventional views of intelligence are based upon inadequate knowledge of the nature of the attributions people make, and moreover, the tests that are based upon these conventional notions usually reflect and perpetuate the existing social order.

Horn is critical of our use of the concept of intelligence, because he believes it represents the reification of a functional unity that does not in fact exist. He argues that what we refer to as intelligence represents a hodgepodge of cognitive capacities, and that our goal should be to try to understand these cognitive capacities rather than to understand an illusory unified capacity that we call intelligence. Horn does believe, however, that there are certain broad abilities that need to be understood in order to comprehend various kinds of intellectual performances, namely, visual thinking, auditory thinking, short-term acquisition-retrieval, long-term retrieval-storage, speediness in reading, correct decisions, attentive speediness, structured knowledge of the culture, and flexibility of reasoning under novel conditions (I-B-1).

Humphreys defines intelligence as the repertoire of intellectual knowledge and skills available to a person at a particular point and time (I-B-1). He believes that the term *intellectual* can be defined only by a consensus of experts. He suggests that it is necessary to understand both the content and the processes of intelligence and that we should understand that intelligence is so complex that any one attempt to describe it or its aspects will be inadequate. He compares us to the proverbial blind men stationed at different parts of an elephant's anatomy, who sought to describe the elephant fully. We, like them, cannot attain such a complete description.

Hunt views intelligence as a shorthand term for the variation in competence on cognitive tasks that is statistically associated with personal variables, either as main effects or as interaction terms (I-B-1). Thus, Hunt defines intelligence in terms of demonstrated individual differences in mental competence. He notes that because variation (individual differences) is a population concept, an individual cannot have "intelligence," although an individual can have specific competencies. Hunt's approach to understanding individual-difference variations is computational. He draws an analogy between the functional architecture and computing of a computer and that of a human. In particular, he believes that intelligence should be understood in terms of the manipulation of symbol systems by the individual. We need to understand both the conscious strategies that people use in manipulating symbols, and the elementary information-processing operations that combine into these strategies (I-B-1-b). Hunt notes that a full understanding of intelligence would require a theory of three levels of performance and their interactions: the level of biology (I-A), the level of elementary information processes (I-B-1-b-i), and the level of both general and specific information-processing strategies (I-B-1-c).

Jensen defines intelligence in terms of the general factor obtained from factoring an intercorrelation matrix of a large number of diverse mental tests. He notes that the tests that load most highly on the general factor usually involve some forms of relation induction or relatively complex mental transformations or manipulations of stimulus input in order to achieve the correct response (I-B-1-b-i-(c); I-B-1-b-i-(d)). He argues that although the general factor that will be obtained differs somewhat from one collection of tests to another, one's goal should be to obtain that general factor from a set of tests that is most highly correlated with the general factors obtained from other sets of tests. Jensen notes that he emphasizes the general factor, rather than group or specific ones, because it is the general factor that proves to be the largest single source of individual differences in all cognitive activities involving some degree of mental complexity that eventuate in behavior that can be measured in terms of some objective standard of performance. He also notes that the general factor carries far more predictive weight than any other single factor or combination of factors in predicting performance in a variety of settings, including both academic (I-C-1) and occupational (I-C-3-a) ones. Jensen believes that intelligence has a biological substrate (I-A), but that it is usefully studied both in the context of laboratory cognitive tasks (I-B-1) and in the context of the everyday environment (II).

Pellegrino argues that in order to understand intelligence, we need to understand the nature of human cognition (I-B-1) as well as the nature of the value system within which that cognition functions (II). He argues that intelligence is implicitly determined by the interaction of the individual's cognitive machinery with that individual's social-cultural environment (III).

In terms of cognition, Pellegrino emphasizes the special importance of metacognitive aspects of mental functioning (I-B-1-a), but these metacognitive processes and contents cannot be understood outside the context of the cognitive processes and contents upon which they act (I-B-1-c).

Scarr notes that the question "What is intelligence?" is actually several questions. A first question pertains to the structure of intelligence, a second to the cognitive processes of intelligence, a third to the neurological processes of intelligence, a fourth to the evolution of intelligence, and a fifth to the sources of individual variability of intelligence (I). Scarr clearly takes a broad rather than narrow view of intelligence, arguing that it is time to conceive of it in terms of people's adaptation in their everyday lives (III). Intelligence requires broad forms of personal adaptation in formulating strategies for solving both the small and the large problems that confront us in our everyday lives.

Schank views intelligence largely in terms of understanding. He suggests that there are three different levels of understanding. The lowest level, making sense, involves finding out events that have taken place and relating them to a perception of the world. For example, reading a newspaper article generally involves what Schank refers to as making sense. Cognitive understanding, the next level, involves building an accurate model of the thought processes of a given person. For example, in reading a set of stories about airplane crashes, one might try to understand the thoughts that went through the heads of the people who were in the plane. Complete empathy, the highest level, involves emotional as well as cognitive understanding. One comprehends not only the thoughts of another, but the person's feelings (I-B-1, I-C-2, I-C-3, III). How can one distinguish between a system that can produce the appearance of understanding and one that truly understands? According to Schank, the key is the ability of a system to explain its own actions. Without such explanations, it is possible that a set of response outputs merely mimics understanding.

Snow presents a definition of intelligence with six aspects: the incorporation of concisely organized knowledge into purposive thinking (I-B-1-b-iii); apprehension of experience (I-B-1-a, I-B-1-b); adaptive purposeful striving (III); fluid-analytical reasoning (I-B-1-b-i-(c)); mental playfulness (I-B-2-b); and idiosyncratic learning (I-B-1-b-i-(b)). Snow notes that these six aspects of intelligence are interactive, working together to produce observable behavior. He does not believe that these six aspects of intelligence constitute necessary or sufficient conditions for intelligence. Rather, he views intelligence as a family resemblance concept, or prototype, which is organized around aspects such as the ones described here.

Sternberg suggests that intelligence should be viewed as mental self-government. He supports his idea by elaborating an analogy between intelligence, on the one hand, and government, on the other. He views intelligence as providing a means to govern ourselves so that our thoughts and actions are organized, coherent, and responsive both to our internally driven needs and to the needs of the environment (I-B, I-C, II, III). In elaborating this analogy, Sternberg attempts to show parallels between intelligence and the functions of government, levels of government, forms of government, scope of government, political spectrum of government, and efficacy of government.

Zigler emphasizes the arbitrary nature of definitions, and the fact that definitions cannot be right or wrong, but only useful or not useful. He views intelligence as a hypothetical construct that has its ultimate reference in the cognitive processes of the individual (I-B-1), but he supports this definition in terms of its usefulness, not in terms of any arbitrary standard of correctness. Zigler also believes that intelligence has a motivational component (I-B-2). As a developmental psychologist, Zigler is particularly interested in the developmental interaction between the individual and the environment (III), and presents a model of the form this interaction takes over time.

To conclude, I have presented in this chapter a framework for characterizing definitions of intelligence, and have applied the framework to the characterization of each of two dozen different definitions of intelligence. Like other frameworks, this one does not capture the richness of detail that inheres in any single definition. It does show, however, the degree to which there exists a consensus among psychologists regarding the broad outlines of a definition of intelligence, and it shows one representation of the form that this consensus takes. In this respect, it shows how quite diverse conceptions of intelligence have a certain basic core that is common to virtually all of them.

PART II

ESSAYS

2.

Intelligence as a Quality of Behavior

Anne Anastasi
Fordham University

Introduction

Intelligence is a word that has been in use over many generations in a human society that has been rapidly evolving, both physically and psychologically. Along the way, the word has acquired many associated meanings, implications, and nuances. It has been widely used in diverse ways in popular speech and in several scholarly disciplines, including philosophy, education, biology, and psychology, among others. It is not surprising, therefore, that when it is presented as a stimulus to a sample of twentieth-century psychologists, it serves as a projective technique. It elicits not a clearly definable concept, but rather an outpouring of the respondent's intellectual goals, aspirations, concerns, and doubts. This was apparent in the 1921 *Journal of Educational Psychology,* survey; I should anticipate a similar result in the present survey.

Nevertheless, certain common trends may be recognized within the diverse responses, trends that reflect the scientific climate of the period. For example, although most of the 1921 respondents called attention to the manifold nature of intelligence and the need for different kinds of intelligence tests to measure different kinds of intelligence, they were still referring to the intelligences required in various contexts within advanced technological societies, as in the United States and Europe. There was little or no evidence of a cross-cultural, worldwide orientation.

The Nature and Measurement of Intelligence

Intelligence is not an entity within the organism but a quality of behavior. Intelligent behavior is essentially adaptive, insofar as it represents effective ways of meeting the demands of a changing environment. Such behavior varies with the species and with the context in which the individual lives. It follows that intelligent behavior (or intelligence) is a pluralistic concept. In simpler organisms, adaptation occurs primarily through biological selection in the species or subspecies—an evolutionary process that is accelerated by short intergeneration time span and abundance of progeny. Adaptation is thus achieved at the expense of excessive waste of individual organisms. At these evolutionary levels, behavior is closely linked with the physical properties of the organism's sensorimotor and connecting equipment; modifiability through learning within the individual's lifetime is at a minimum. In higher forms, the relative contribution of natural selection and learning is progressively reversed.

In the human species, the influence of learning on intelligent behavior has been immensely enhanced through the intergenerational cultural transmission of a rapidly mounting accumulation of knowledge. This influence has been further strengthened through the organized transmission of knowledge provided by systems of formal schooling. Within the human species, intelligence comprises that combination of cognitive skills and knowledge demanded, fostered, and rewarded by the particular culture within which the individual becomes socialized.

Individual differences in human intelligence can be measured at different levels of generality or specificity, depending upon the purpose of the assessment. At a relatively broad level, we find the traditional "intelligence tests," which can be more accurately described as measures of academic intelligence or scholastic aptitude. They measure a kind of intelligent behavior that is both developed by formal schooling and required for progress along the academic ladder. There is a large body of data, derived from both clinical observation and validation studies against academic and occupational criteria, which demonstrates that the particular combination of cognitive skills and knowledge sampled by these tests plays a significant part in much of what goes on in modern technologically advanced societies. For fuller assessment of an individual's readiness to perform in particular occupations or courses of study, tests of separate abilities in such areas as the verbal, mathematical, spatial, mechanical, or perceptuo-motor are useful; still more narrowly defined skills and knowledge may be required for the execution of clearly defined tasks, as in certain military occupational specialties.

In other cultures, other comparable hierarchies of intellectual behavior could be identified, although in the absence of formal systems of schooling it is unlikely that very broad factors or widely generalizable cognitive skills would emerge. When individuals or groups are endeavoring to move from one culture to another (as in developing nations), tests designed within the new or target culture can assess readiness for such a move, while information about the initial or background culture can help in understanding the individual's current intellectual status.

Crucial Next Steps in Research

There are several lines of research that would increase our understanding of the nature and etiology of human intelligence. In most of these, only meager beginnings have been made thus far.

There is need for more research on the *qualitative changes in intelligence with age.* Studies on infants have provided suggestive results about age-linked competencies and about developmental transformation in the common factors identified at different ages. Changes in factor patterns and in the composition of intelligence among older children and adults are also relevant.

From another angle, there is a dearth of information on the characteristic *environmental demands* encountered by different groups classified by age levels, cultures, subcultures, or other experiential categories. The development of indigenous tests to sample culturally significant behavioral constructs, followed by factor analyses of the test results, should contribute substantially to an understanding of cognitive trait formation.

More information is needed on the role of *formal schooling,* with its separation in time and place from everyday-life contexts, in the development of concept formation and abstract thinking skills. A related question pertains to the contribution of *content knowledge* to intelligent behavior, as well as to the relation of content to specific intellectual skills.

Research on the *processes* individuals follow to solve intellectual problems has been approached from a variety of angles, as illustrated by direct questioning, analysis of errors, administration of Piagetian tasks, and some of the more sophisticated techniques of contemporary cognitive psychology. Such approaches should contribute to the development of assessment procedures better suited to the diagnosis and remediation of intellectual difficulties.

Finally, all tests should be fitted within a framework of *cultural diversity.* No test is—or should be—culture-free, because human behavior is not culture-free. For most practical purposes, the most effective tests are likely to be those developed for clearly defined purposes and for use within specified contexts. Although these contexts will vary in breadth, none is likely to cover the entire human species. The important point is to identify the locus and range of cultural (or other experiential) context for which any given test is appropriate and then to keep both the use of the test and the interpretation of its scores within those contextual boundaries.

3.

Notes on the Concept of Intelligence

Paul B. Baltes

**Max Planck Institute for Human Development
and Education, Berlin**

My current views on the concept of human intelligence—after close to two decades of research on intelligence from a psychometric and life-span developmental point of view—have been enriched recently by cognitive psychology and developmental pragmatics (Baltes, Dittmann-Kohli, & Dixon, 1984; Dixon & Baltes, in press). This brief biographical observation implies that my own beliefs about the concept of intelligence have undergone some significant changes.

On Definition: Theoretical Construct Versus Field of Study

When defining a concept such as intelligence, the scientific expectation is that the concept entails some fairly robust essentials that constitute its theoretical core (Brandtstädter, 1982). The scientific practice of conceptualizing and measuring intelligence with its multiple and myriad approaches has persuaded me, however, that the theoretical core of intelligence—beyond its substantive focus on the structure and function of the mind—cannot be delineated in a clear and widely acceptable fashion. Surplus meaning, as well as operational, theoretical, and metatheoretical disagreement, exist to such an extent that the concept of intelligence is not a single theoretical construct. Rather, what seems to be indicated by intelligence is a "fuzzy" set of partly irreconcilable concepts, ideas, and research questions.

Aside from issues of theoretical clarity and precision, there is also the question of manageable scope. The problem of scope of intelligence as a superconstruct is illustrated by the recurring posture—dating back at least to Quetelet's (1835) account—to have intelligence encompass not only the mechanics and basic architecture of cognitive functioning, but also (a) knowledge and (b) motivational achievement factors. Making these an intrinsic part of the core of intelligence is running the risk of giving up any reasonable specificity that intelligence may possess as a theoretical construct. An alternative theoretical approach is to acknowledge the relevance of these factors but to locate them not in the theoretical core of intelligence, but in the system context of intellectual functioning.

My general approach to this state of affairs is not one of exasperation or despair. Rather, I take it as an index of (a) the large territory that questions about human intelligence cover, and (b) the need, not for a unified model or theory, but for further specification of subterritories or subconstructs. Whether these subterritories can be linked together now or later into a multilevel or overarching theory of intelligence is of lesser significance. The effort to try for a unified theory is commendable. Its possible accomplishment, however, is not a necessary condition for good psychological theory or theories about intelligence.

The ensuing proposal regarding the definition of intelligence is twofold: First, intelligence should not be used as a "theoretical" construct, but as the label for a field of scholarship. This field is characterized by the study of factors, mechanisms, and abilities associated with cognitive achievement involving the mind as a central locus of operation. Second, if one is interested in formulating theoretical accounts of facets of the field, then it is necessary to introduce qualifiers to be added to the term *intelligence*. Otherwise, surplus meaning and metatheoretical discord will continue to be paramount.

For example, rather than speak of intelligence per se, my preference is to speak of constructs such as innate intellectual capacity (*Anlage*), intellectual reserve capacity, learning capacity, intellectual abilities, intelligent systems, problem-solving ability, and knowledge systems. Each of these compound terms permits the generation of more theoretical specificity and precision. No claim is made that any of the subconstructs marks the entire domain of intelligence, nor that together they form the coherent body of a unified theory. However, it is expected that the specification of subconstructs permits systematic building of "microtheory" with an acceptable measure of theoretical clarity and precision. Subsequently it may be possible to link such microtheoretical accounts into a theoretical network, perhaps of the fuzzy-set kind. Moreover, when following this strategy of microtheoretical elaboration, it is possible to attend to each subconstruct within varying and occasionally diverse theoretical and methodological paradigms that are suitable to the task. Examples include the use of physiological measures if the search is one for biological origins; the application of heredity-environment designs if the central question deals with the environmental versus genetic location of interindividual differences; the use of learning designs if the primary interest is in the understanding of intellectual reserve capacity and the acquisition of cognitive skills; or the use of cognitive-science methodology if one is interested in the mapping of factual and procedural knowledge systems.

On Research Priorities

In addition to supporting the widely endorsed quest to achieve better convergence between product-oriented (mostly correlational) and process-oriented (mostly experimental) work (Keating, 1984), three strands of research programs are my favorites: (a) the study of intraindividual plasticity; (b) elaboration of the concept of crystallized intelligence into the study of knowledge systems and the pragmatics of intelligence; and (c) integrative formulation of life-span developmental conceptions of intelligence.

Intraindividual change and plasticity. The study of intraindividual processes and plasticity is the first cornerstone of future research. In the psychometric study of abilities, for example, we need as much a theory about the measurement of the true "trait" score(s) of persons as we need theory and measurement of true "changeability" or plasticity scores (Lerner, 1984). The application of testing-the-limits strategies and learning diagnostics, for example, is very underdeveloped in the area of intelligence testing (Guthke, 1982; Wiedl, 1984). Similarly, when it comes to the understanding of the origins and formation of interindividual differences in mental abilities, we need to recognize that interindividual differences are always the outcome of differing intraindividual change patterns (Baltes, Cornelius, & Nesselroade, 1978). The royal road toward the understanding of interindividual differences is intraindividual change and differences therein, and not the reverse, which is the more typical strategy associated with the psychometric tradition. In the same vein, I am persuaded that the intensive, single-subject study of how individuals build up and transform systems of factual and procedural knowledge is a promising avenue toward capturing the structure and function of mind. Research conducted using this person- and process-oriented strategy can exemplify how, and under what conditions, processes of acquisition, maintenance, transformation, and loss of cognitive skills and knowledge systems occur in principle.

From crystallized intelligence to the pragmatics of intelligence. A second research priority deals with a vigorous refinement and expansion of our knowledge about the content of intellect and its pragmatic use at different locations and times of life. My own preference is to separate, as clearly as possible in such research, the "content-free" mechanics of intelligence from the content- and context-related pragmatics of intelligence (Baltes et al., 1984). After this separation has been accomplished, it may lead to subsequent integrative scholarship designed to show how the mechanics and pragmatics interrelate when put into joint operation.

Cattell's and Horn's (Cattell, 1971; Horn, 1982) distinction between fluid and crystallized intelligence is a useful step in that direction. However, conceptualization and measurement of crystallized intelligence (in terms of both its generalized and its specialized aspects) lag far behind conceptualization and measurement of fluid intelligence. What seems desirable is to recast the conception of crystallized intelligence by application of methodology provided by the cognitive-pyschological study of knowledge systems and by more systematic consideration of the ecological contexts and cognitive demands of everyday life. This will permit us to move beyond the content territory charted by the world of the school and academia to include, for example, domains of the social and professional world.

Development and aging of intelligence. The research avenues outlined need to be placed into the framework of lifelong development. In the final analysis, it is the developmental account of the structure and function of intelligence in the life course that makes for a complete story of the field. Life-span research on intelligence addresses such questions as how intelligence develops, how it is organized, how it operates as a system requiring continuing adaptive functioning, where interindividual differences come from, how individuals deal with aging losses in selected aspects of intellectual reserve capacity (plasticity), as well as how transfer from one life domain to another occurs or does not occur.

Personally, I am most intrigued by two emerging research approaches in this area. A first deals with the question of limits of functioning. I expect a testing-the-limits strategy to yield more systematic knowledge about the course and range of development, as well as about the cognitive components involved, than is presently available (Kliegl & Baltes, in preparation). A second largely unexplored area concerns the study of substitutive and compensatory factors and mechanisms in intellectual productions. Especially in the second half of life, I expect the strategic use of substitutive factors and compensatory skills to become a hallmark of continued efficacy. At present, we have little knowledge about the self-generated prosthetics and specializations of intellectual efficacy.

REFERENCES

Baltes, P.B., Dittmann-Kohli, F., & Dixon, R.A. (1984). New perspectives on the development of intelligence in adulthood: Toward a dual-process conception and a model of selective optimization with compensation. In P.B. Baltes & O.G. Brim, Jr. (Eds.), *Life-span development and behavior* (Vol. 6, pp. 33–76). New York: Academic Press.

Baltes, P.B., Nesselroade, J.R., & Cornelius, S.W. (1978). Multivariate antecedents of structural change in development: A simulation of cumulative environmental patterns. *Multivariate Behavioral Research, 13,* 127–152.

Brandtstädter, J. (1982). Apriorische Elemente in psychologischen Forschungsprogrammen. *Zeitschrift für Sozialpsychologie, 13,* 267–277.

Cattell, R.B. (1971). *Abilities: Structure, growth and action.* Boston: Houghton Mifflin.

Dixon, R.A., & Baltes, P.B. (in press). Toward life-span research on the functions and pragmatics of intelligence. In R.J. Sternberg & R.K. Wagner (Eds.), *Practical intelligence: Origins of competence in the everyday world.* New York: Cambridge University Press.

Guthke, J. (1982). The learning concept—An alternative to the traditional static intelligence test. *The German Journal of Psychology, 6,* 306–324.

Horn, J.L. (1982). The aging of human abilities. In B.B. Wolman (Ed.), *Handbook of developmental psychology* (pp. 847–870). Englewood Cliffs, NJ: Prentice-Hall.

Keating, D.P. (1984). The emperor's new clothes: The "new look" in intelligence research. In R.J. Sternberg (Ed.), *Advances in the psychology of human intelligence* (Vol. 2, pp. 1–45). Hillsdale, NJ: Erlbaum.

Kliegl, R., & Baltes, P.B. (in preparation). Theory-guided analysis of aging mechanisms through research on expertise and testing-the-limits. In C. Schooler & K.W. Schaie (Eds.), *Social structure and intellectual functioning in adulthood and old age.*

Lerner, R.M. (1984). *On the nature of human plasticity.* New York: Cambridge University Press.

Quetelet, A. (1835). Sur l'homme et la développement des ses facultés. Paris: Bachelier. (Published in English in 1824)

Wiedl, K.H. (1984). Lerntests: Nur Forschungsmittel und Forschungsgegenstand? *Zeitschrift für Entwicklungspsychologie und Pädagogische Psychologie, 16,* 245–281.

4.

Capacities, Dispositions, and Rational Thinking

Jonathan Baron

University of Pennsylvania

.

I define intelligence (in Baron, 1985a, chapter 1) as the set of whatever abilities make people successful at achieving their rationally chosen goals, whatever those goals might be, and whatever environment they are in (provided it is a real one rather than one that is constructed only to prove my definition unworkable). These component abilities are defined within a theory of mental processes, which then becomes part of a theory of intelligence. To say that a person has a certain level of an ability is to say that he or she can meet a certain standard of speed, accuracy, or appropriateness in a component process defined by the theory in question.

There are two types of abilities: *Capacities,* which are things like mental speed, mental energy, or retrieval accuracy (holding trace strength constant), cannot be increased by instruction or self-instruction at the moment. The definition allows capacities to be affected by practice, but I argue (Baron, 1985b) that none is. Unpracticeable capacities are the "hard-wired" components of intelligence, and together they may be said to constitute "narrow intelligence." *Dispositions,* such as the disposition to search thoroughly before being satisfied with one's solution to a problem, or the disposition to be self-critical, may be controlled by instruction. It will not help to tell a person to increase his or her working memory capacity, but it might help to tell that person to be more thorough or more self-critical.

In order to play the role I have assigned them, components of intelligence must be general, that is, they must affect performance in a sufficient variety of situations so that we can expect them to affect success in some situations in any realistic environment or culture. The important point here is that the component must be definable across situations. Generality in this sense does not imply correlations across situations in which a component is manifest. For example, if we teach a person to be more self-critical in schoolwork, the change need not transfer automatically to personal decision-making. Whether a disposition is general across domains or not may well depend on how we teach it. For capacities, the question of generality is an empirical one (see Baron & Treiman, 1980).

Many of the dispositional components of intelligence may be subsumed under a conception of *rational thinking* (Baron, 1985a). Violation of the constraints of rationality, by definition, is likely to lead to failure to conform to certain normative models, which anyone, on reflection, would want to follow: For example, one would want to avoid courses of action that are undesirable, taking into account all of one's relevant values (including the values concerned with the time and effort put into thinking itself). Some methods of thinking, certain heuristics for example, might be better than others, on the average, at avoiding this kind of mistake. I have argued that thinking is irrationally conducted if there is too little (or too much) search for possibilities, evidence, and goals, or if there is too little (or too much) self-criticism in the search for and use of evidence. For example, it is probably irrational, in most cases, to make important decisions by "intuition," considering only a single possibility, when there is plenty of time to consider other possibilities and relevant evidence. There does not have to be a single best way to think rationally. Several different ways might be appropriate. If people conduct their thinking rationally, they need not blame their thinking for any errors or misfortunes that result, for they will have done the best they could, given what they knew at the time.

The concept I have outlined makes it virtually impossible to measure intelligence *exactly* with a group test or any other sort of test. Even if we had a complete list of the components of intelligence, we would not know how they should be weighed relative to one another for any individual. Each component is supposed to be important to some degree, but component A may be very important for one person, and component B, for another, given the goals these people would choose. Furthermore, it is unlikely that components are completely general, and the material we use to measure a component may be a relatively poor indicator of the level of that component with other material. Finally, there may be more than one correct way to specify the list of components.

Although we cannot measure intelligence exactly, we can measure it approximately. If we make up a battery of component measures, it is virtually certain that the total score on this test will *correlate* with true intelligence (as it might be defined, say, for sets of people with identical goals). This is because we have ensured (by definition) that the components of intelligence are to some extent useful to anyone, and although we cannot guarantee perfect generality across material, there is likely to be *some* generality.

The most direct way to make up such an (imperfect) test of intelligence is to devise measures of theoretically defined components (as done by Sternberg, 1985) rather than target performances. One requirement of such measures is that they be unaffected by specific knowledge (e.g., of vocabulary or facts), for such knowledge is too specific to count as part of intelligence. One way to avoid contamination by specific knowledge is to use two tasks to measure each component, an experimental task that is sensitive to the component in question, and a control task that is like the experimental task, except that it is less sensitive (Baron & Treiman, 1980). It must usually be demonstrated that the measure derived from comparison of these two tasks is not affected by irrelevant causal factors (such as specific knowledge, or components other than the one being measured). Part of the validation of such a test would involve experiments on the generality of the components across different material. It might also be worthwhile to ask whether components are valid constructs, in the sense of Cronbach and Meehl (1955), across different kinds of material. (We must bear in mind, however, that the generality of dispositional components might increase if efforts were made to teach such components more generally.)

If we want such a test, we are not far from having it, I would think. In fact, we might develop several different tests based on different lists of components. One test that approaches my ideal—in its use of difference scores to assess theoretically specified components—is the Prototype Test of Decoding Skills (Adams et al., 1980), although this test is limited to reading.

However, do we want such a test? What would it do for us that current tests do not already do, given that it would only be approximate in any case? Rather than a single global test of theoretically defined intelligence, it might be better to have different tests for different purposes. For example, we might want a test of narrow intelligence (the uncontrollable part) for the diagnosis of retardation and dementia and for evaluation of their medical treatment. The steps involved in construction and validation of such a test would be much like those I described, but for a narrower purpose.

If we want a test to determine educational placement, perhaps the best test is one that simulates different types of instruction for a short time (like those advocated by Campione, Brown, & Ferrara, 1982, and Feuerstein, 1979). Here, the type of research needed is the sort used to look for aptitude-treatment interactions, for the usual reasons (Snow & Yalow, 1982).

If we want a test to evaluate the thinking of a student or a group of students, so that we know where to put our educational efforts, we need tests that are sensitive to the quality of thinking in a variety of domains. In a test battery based on this principle, we might ask a subject to study a novel concept and paraphrase what he or she has learned, to learn and carry out a novel procedure (either from instructions or by trial and error), to evaluate arguments for their soundness and criticize their flaws, to make an argument, to construct a small work of art out of limited materials, to respond to personal and moral dilemmas (Brim, Glass, Lavin, & Goodman, 1962; Colby, Kohlberg, Gibbs, & Lieberman, 1983), or to solve dynamic problems (Dörner & Reither, 1978). Success in such tasks is likely to be more predictive (than current tests) of success in the wide range of situations that occur in people's real plans. The use of a variety of materials can detect a weakness in a particular dispositional component across many domains, or in a single domain across many components. The design and scoring of such a test requires ingenuity, as it is necessary to observe not just correctness but also the way in which the subject does the task. We need to know what heuristics a subject uses, and we need to be able to detect failures to think of some relevant possibility, piece of evidence, or goal that the subject could have thought of. Think-aloud protocols can be useful here (Baron, 1985a, chapter 3), but for group tests, less direct methods might be needed (e.g., Sternberg & Powell, 1983). Written productions can also be coded for certain types of errors (Perkins, Allen, & Hafner, 1983).

Research relevant to such an enterprise would concern not only the design and evaluation of tests, but also the study of prevalent heuristics and biases in thinking (Baron, 1985a; Kruglanski & Ajzen, 1983; Nisbett & Ross, 1980; Perkins et al., 1983). The study of heuristics and biases is not a purely empirical matter but also a philosophical one, for we need to decide what a bias *is;* and it is a matter of design as well, for whether a heuristic is good not for a given task depends on whether we can improve on it. This sort of research would be valuable not only for the development of tests but also for the design of new educational methods. Indeed, the study of intelligence as something we should teach may be as important as the study of intelligence as something we measure (Baron, 1981).

Here is a final suggestion. Could we think of the part of intelligence concerned with good thinking as a criterion-referenced concept rather than a continuum of individual differences? By this account, an intelligent person would be one who always knows whether he or she understands something or not, and who would never solve certain problems (e.g., in logic or mathematics) incorrectly while being 100% confident of being correct. For other types of problems, such as those in morals or politics, a good thinker would always remain open to new possibilities, evidence, and goals, would always seek evidence on both sides (at least for a short time); and would never be certain that improvement in judgment was impossible. When given sufficient time to make an important decision, a good thinker would always look for other possibilities and for criticisms of the first possibility to enter his or her mind. An interesting exercise is to imagine what the world would be like if schools throughout the world regarded it as part of their mission to ensure that everyone could pass a test based on this idea.

REFERENCES

Adams, M.J., Huggins, A.W.F., Starr, B.J., Rollins, A.M., Zuckerman, L.E., Stevens, K.N., & Nickerson, R.S. (1980). *A prototype test of decoding skills* (Report No. 4316). Cambridge, MA: Bolt Beranek & Newman.

Baron, J. (1981). Reflective thinking as a goal of education. *Intelligence, 5,* 291–309.

Baron, J. (1985a). *Rationality and intelligence.* Cambridge, England: Cambridge University Press.

Baron, J. (1985b). What kinds of intelligence components are fundamental? In J. Segal, S. Chipman, & R. Glaser (Eds.), *Thinking and learning skills: Vol. 2. Current research and open questions.* Hillsdale, NJ: Erlbaum.

Baron, J., & Treiman, R. (1980). Some problems in the study of differences in cognitive processes. *Memory and Cognition, 8,* 313–321.

Brim, O.G., Glass, D.C., Lavin, D.E., & Goodman, N. (1962). *Personality and decision processes.* Stanford, CA: Stanford University Press.

Campione, J.C., Brown, A.L., & Ferrara, R.A. (1982). Mental retardation and intelligence. In R.J. Sternberg (Ed.), *Handbook of human intelligence* (pp. 392–490). Cambridge, England: Cambridge University Press.

Colby, A., Kohlberg, L., Gibbs, J., & Lieberman, M. (1983). A longitudinal study of moral judgment. *Monographs of the Society for Research in Child Development, 48,* (1–2, Serial No. 200).

Cronbach, L.J., & Meehl, P.E. (1955). Construct validity in psychological tests. *Psychological Bulletin, 52,* 281–302.

Dörner, D., & Reither, F. (1978). Über das Problemlösen in sehr komplexen Realitätsbereichen. *Zeitschrift für Experimentelle und Angewandte Psychologie, 25,* 527–551.

Feuerstein, R. (1979). *The dynamic assessment of retarded performance: The learning potential assessment device, theory, instruments, and techniques.* Baltimore, MD: University Park Press.

Kruglanski, A.W., & Ajzen, I. (1983). Bias and error in human judgment. *European Journal of Social Psychology, 13,* 1–44.

Nisbett, R., & Ross, L. (1980). *Human inference: Strategies and shortcomings of social judgment.* Englewood Cliffs, NJ: Prentice-Hall.

Perkins, D.N., Allen, R., & Hafner, J. (1983). Difficulties in everyday reasoning. In W. Maxwell (Ed.), *Thinking: The expanding frontier* (pp. 177–189). Philadelphia, PA: Franklin Institute.

Snow, R.E., & Yalow, E. (1982). Education and intelligence. In R.J. Sternberg (Ed.), *Handbook of human intelligence* (pp. 493–585). Cambridge, England: Cambridge University Press.

Sternberg, R.J. (1985). *Beyond IQ: A triarchic theory of human intelligence.* Cambridge, England: Cambridge University Press.

Sternberg, R.J., & Powell, J.S. (1983). Comprehending verbal comprehension. *American Psychologist, 38,* 878–893.

5.

A Cross-Cultural View of Intelligence

J. W. Berry

**Queen's University
Kingston, Canada**

From my point of view as a cross-cultural psychologist, the two questions which have been posed are very much related to each other. For reasons outlined below, I conceive of *intelligence,* as presently used in psychology, to be a culture-bound, ethnocentric, and excessively narrow construct. In contrast, I consider that after certain "next steps" are accomplished, there may prove to exist a pan-human, universal, and broader construct that applies to intellectual functioning in the species as a whole. Since my present views are a coalition and synthesis of arguments and data I have earlier expressed, I will refer to these, in part to document their origin, and in part to assist any reader who may wish to obtain a fuller presentation.

At the present time *intelligence* is a construct which refers to the end product of individual development in the cognitive-psychological domain (as distinct from the affective and conative domains); this includes sensory and perceptual functioning, but excludes motor, motivational, emotional, and social functioning. (Its assessment, of course, can inadvertently include all of these latter.) I consider that intelligence is adaptive for the cultural group, in the sense that it develops to permit the group to operate effectively in a particular ecological context; it is also adaptive for the individual, permitting people to operate in their particular cultural and ecological contexts.

Given that the construct has been conceptualized in one cultural area of the world (Euroamerican), and that it is operationalized by tasks cognitively valued in that same context, the cross-culturalist is likely to ask whether other peoples might conceptualize cognitive competence in somewhat different terms; they may also ask whether other peoples might develop themselves toward those competencies, and assess members of their own group according to their attainment of these competencies. My own answer is yes to all these questions, and I believe that the important "next steps" for psychology should be to obtain evidence regarding the validity of this view.

The evolution of my position can be recounted succinctly. In my first field study (Berry, 1966), I found wide differences in performance on perceptual and cognitive tasks between two groups carrying out their lives in widely differing fashions (Arctic hunter-gatherers and African agriculturalists). But they could not, on any sensible basis, be said to differ in general intelligence: Both groups were obviously carrying out competent lives in their own ecological contexts. This led me to the conclusion that different groups are likely to conceptualize and develop their own "intelligence" in quite different ways (see Berry, 1984, for a review of this proposition). On the basis of further studies in other societies (Berry, 1971), I argued for a position of "radical cultural relativism" (Berry, 1972) with respect to the construct of intelligence: As psychologists, we should admit that we do not know in any absolute or a priori sense what intelligence is in other cultures, and until we do, we should not use *our* construct to describe *their* cognitive competencies, nor *our* tests to measure *them.* My 1976 book attempted to assemble the first decade of work, and proposed two basic hypotheses. First, it was argued that an ecological model which incorporates cultural group adaptation to recurrent problems encountered in the daily lives of group members could predict what kinds of cognitive abilities would be developed in a population (see Berry, 1980, for a specific operational model and Berry & Irvine, in press, for a recent review of day-to-day cognitive performance). Second, it was proposed that we should conceive of the resulting phenomena as variable patterns of abilities ("cognitive styles") which are differentially developed and deployed in different cultural groups according to their ecological and cultural contexts (see Berry et al., in press, for an empirical test of this hypothesis).

From the above brief tour, a number of "next steps" can be extracted and made explicit:

1. Psychology should no longer bother to document the by now obvious fact that *they* cannot perform *our* tests; continuing to use our tests is not likely to reveal what they *can* do, as opposed to what they *cannot* do.
2. Psychology should carry out *ecological analyses* of what the cognitive demands are of living in their ecological contexts. Such a "job analysis" could identify the tasks which need to be accomplished by them, and the cognitive abilities valued by the population, toward which cogni-

tion is socialized and developed. This type of analysis would also include a search for the existence of indigenous concepts of competence, and their meanings and components.

3. Psychology should attempt to operationalize these competencies, employing both our own technical disciplinary accomplishments in assessing performance, and their concepts and performances in cognitive (and perhaps in related) domains.

4. Psychology should, when 2 and 3 are accomplished, attempt to assemble the resulting information (including our own concepts and performances) into a universal theory of cognitive competence which would be appropriate for all peoples.

It is, of course, not possible to predict what such a new theory would be like in any detail, but some hints are already available. First, indigenous conceptions do not limit themselves strictly to the cognitive domain; there is a frank recognition that social, affective, and motivational factors are necessarily involved in cognitive performances. Second, the "fast, analytic" flavor of our current notion of intelligence is not universal; even on the basis of our limited current knowledge, there is evidence for a "paced, deliberate, social" conception and practice which is highly valued and widely accepted in other societies. Third, given these two initial indications, we are unlikely to be able to retain any single factor or unidimensional construct which will be valid for understanding or measuring intelligence (or whatever we eventually call it) among all the world's peoples.

These observations raise fundamental problems for the unity of the construct of *intelligence* as it is now generally used in Euroamerican psychology. The loss of such a construct, of course, does not mean that we cannot attain other descriptions which apply universally to the developed abilities of humankind. It is, in fact, the pursuit of such new, pan-human, constructs which cross-cultural psychology sets as its ultimate goal.

REFERENCES

Berry, J.W. (1966). Temne and Eskimo perceptual skills. *International Journal of Psychology, 1*, 207–229.

Berry, J.W. (1971). Ecological and cultural factors in perceptual development. *Canadian Journal of Behavioural Science, 3*, 324–336.

Berry, J.W. (1972). Radical cultural relativism and the concept of intelligence. In L.J. Cronbach and P.J. Drenth (Eds.), *Mental tests and cultural adaptation* (pp. 77–88). The Hague: Mouton.

Berry, J.W. (1976). *Human ecology and cognitive style: Studies in cultural and psychological adaptation.* New York: Sage/Halsted.

Berry, J.W. (1980). Ecological analyses for cross-cultural psychology. In N. Warren (Ed.), *Studies in cross-cultural psychology* (pp. 157–189). London: Academic Press.

Berry, J.W. (1984). Towards a universal psychology of cognitive competence. *International Journal of Psychology, 19,* 335–361.

Berry, J.W., and Irvine, S.H. (in press). Bricolage: Savages do it daily. In R.J. Sternberg and R. Wagner (Eds.), *Practical intelligence: Origins of competence in the everyday world.* New York: Cambridge University Press.

Berry, J.W., van de Koppel, J., Sénéchal, C., Annis, R.C., Bahuchet, S., Cavalli-Sforza, L.L., and Witkin, H.A. (in press). *On the edge of the forest: Cultural adaptation and cognitive development in Central Africa.* Lisse: Swets and Zeitlinger.

6.

Academic Intelligence and Learning Potential

Ann L. Brown
Joseph C. Campione
University of Illinois

The Nature and Measurement of Intelligence

What is intelligence? Can intelligence be measured? These are no less important and controversial issues today than they were in the original 1921 symposium, "Intelligence and Its Measurement." And no less difficult to answer. To render the assignment somewhat manageable, we decided to concentrate on just one form of intelligence and one potential candidate for underlying process: academic intelligence and learning mechanisms. This was a "hot" topic in the early part of the century, although contemporary views are more aware of the complexity of multiple intelligences—polymorphously determined qualities that are elusive indeed to define, explain, and measure. Thus, while denying that academic intelligence is the only form, or even a privileged form, of intelligence, and that learning and transfer mechanisms are the only, or even privileged, underlying mechanisms, we concentrate on these issues because of their controversial history since 1921.

   Given their greater faith in one robust faculty, "the intellect," psychologists in the early part of the century were much more confident in the existence of a single determinant, or a few major determinants, of intelligence. One of the favorite candidates in the 1921 Symposium was *the ability to learn.* Colvin described intelligence as "equivalent to the

capacity to learn." Pinter defined it as "the ability to adapt adequately to
relatively new situations" and as "the ease of forming new habits." Herman
described the intelligent man as "one who is capable of readily appropriat-
ing information or knowledge—intelligence involves two factors—the capacity for knowledge and knowledge possessed." And Dearborn quite explicitly dubbed intelligence as "the capacity to learn or profit from
experience." We will illustrate the changing fortunes of this position
through consideration of two programs of research, our own and that of
Woodrow, a protagonist in 1921.

Woodrow, like others in the 1921 symposium defined intelligence as
"the capacity to acquire capacity," and he undertook a series of studies
between 1917 and 1940 to determine whether learning and transfer efficiency were related to standard IQ measures. For example, in 1917 Woodrow published two papers concerning the learning (Woodrow, 1917a) and
transfer (Woodrow, 1917b) performance of normal and retarded students
matched for a mental age of nine to ten years. The learning tasks involved a
geometrical-form sorting situation in which the subjects were required to
sort five forms into different boxes. The students sorted 500 of these a day
for 13 days, with the order of the boxes changed every two days. The main
metric was the increase over time in the number of forms sorted (error
rates were very low). Transfer tests consisted of two new sorting tasks
(lengths of sticks and colored pegs) and two cancellation tasks (letters and
geometric forms). No difference in learning and transfer between the normal and retarded samples was found. In subsequent work with college
students (Woodrow, 1938a, 1938b), learning was assessed on tasks such as
backward writing, reproduction of spot patterns, horizontal adding, cancel-
ing letters, estimating lengths, and speed in making gates (making four
horizontal lines and one diagonal slash in each square of a page divided into
1,000 squares). Transfer measures were not included because by the 1930s
learning theorists, indoctrinated by Thorndike, were quite convinced that
transfer hardly ever happens! Again Woodrow found no intelligence-learning relation at all. Reviewing the contemporary literature, Woodrow denied
the intelligence-learning position so popular in 1921, when he stated that
"intelligence, far from being identical with the amount of improvement
shown by practice, has practically nothing to do with the matter" (Woodrow 1946). This conclusion, without consideration for the type of research
that supported it, took over the status of doctrine for 25 years.

Woodrow's theory of learning was typical of the associationist, general
process theories of the 1930–1950 period. It was not a theory of active un-
destanding, but one of the passive formation of associative connections via
the mechanisms of recency, contiguity, and the law of effect. The learning-
transfer process was seen as an extremely general one that could be tapped
in any task domain. Within this tradition, the most common measure of

learning efficiency was the number of reinforced trials it took for an individual to reach some criterion, or the amount of improvement that could be brought about by practice.

In contrast, contemporary learning theories are theories of understanding that admit privileged classes of learning and that cede a special place to the learner's understanding and control of the learning process—metacognition, if you will. Contemporary work is guided by a view of learning as an active, socially mediated process. Great care in task analysis is seen as a necessary condition for evaluating learning and transfer, which are assumed to operate within limited domains. The problems to be learned are set in nonarbitrary domains, that is, ones where there are rules for the students to learn and where it is possible to come to understand why certain responses are appropriate in given situations and not in others. This understanding then serves as a basis for subsequent use of the newly acquired information; in other words, principled transfer is possible. The preferred metric of learning is a change in learning processes rather than an increase in products or speed of production over time. Often, this change in process is socially mediated via a supportive context that involves relatively direct instruction.

Guided by such a learning theory, in a series of recent studies we have consistently found a clear relation between psychometric IQ and learning or transfer efficiency (Brown & Campione, 1984; Campione & Brown, 1984). The tasks involved IQ test–like items, progressive matrix and series completion problems that permit principled transfer, that is, the problems could differ in surface formats but still obey the same underlying set of basic rules. Aid was given if independent solution was not obtained, with the aid proceeding from very minimal, general prompts to more and more specific hints to solution. Estimated was the minimum amount of aid needed before independent performance was achieved. Our findings are diametrically opposed to Woodrow's. In comparative studies of normal and retarded children, also matched for an MA of 9–10 years, normal children outperformed retarded learners, and the magnitude of this difference increased as the similarity of the learning and transfer contexts decreased. In other studies involving a wide spread of normal ability, learning and transfer metrics were significantly correlated with IQ. Furthermore, if one considers "domain-specific" improvement, that is the difference between pre- and post-test performance measures, even after IQ and pretest levels were statistically removed, a considerable amount of the variance in improvement was attributable to the amount of aid needed to learn and to transfer, approximately 20% in each case. Alternatively, if one looks at simple correlations, the best predictor of improvement from the pretest to the post-test was performance on far transfer items, followed by near transfer indices and then learning efficiency. The conclusion is that individual differences in

learning and transfer performance are related to IQ and are important pre-
dictors of performance within a domain.

We argue that the differences between Woodrow's results and ours
reflect quite disparate theoretical conceptions of what learning is, conceptions that dictate what form of learning is examined. Woodrow's theory led
him to concentrate on increased speed of production following practice.
Our theory led us to consider the amount of help needed for the acquisition
and application of a set of rules, rather than the number of trials required for
learning to appear.

Another feature of our work is the concentration on current learning,
rather than the fruits of past learning, a development recommended in the
1921 symposium by Woodrow, Dearborn, Haggerty, Colvin, and others, all
of whom made the point that IQ tests, as a measure of past learning, were
only indirectly a measure of current learning ability. Such tests provide a
good measure of learning ability only if one makes the tenuous assumption
that all tested persons have had "common opportunities for past learning"
(Colvin). All argued that better yet would be a measure of learning as it is
actually occurring, in other words, dynamic rather than static, prospective
rather than retrospective, indices of learning. These views resonate well to
contemporary approaches to learning and dynamic assessment influenced
by Vygotsky's (1978) theory of psychosocial development.

Next Steps in Research

Implicit in all the existing work, however, is an assumption of a general
learning facility that is reflected catholically across domains. But even in the
1921 symposium there was controversy concerning the existence of *g.*
"The child who is the best of a thousand at his age at the undoubtedly
intellectual task of mental multiplication will not be the best at the equally
indubitably intellectual task of thinking out verbal puzzles" (Thorndike).
Keeping in mind that prediction of academic performance was the guiding
force behind the architecture of IQ tests, and furthermore that prediction
should inform remediation—". . . *après le mal, le remede*" (Binet, 1909)—
a consideration of learning and transfer status within specific domains
should improve prediction, and more importantly, prescriptions for
remediation.

The enormous advances in our understanding of learning in traditional
academic domains of mathematics, science, writing, and reading, spurred by
the emergent discipline of cognitive science, enables us to consider domain-specific indices of learning potential in a manner never before possible. And there are considerable advantages to developing procedures for
estimating readiness to acquire information in an academic domain such as

elementary arithmetic or algebra. If data comparable to those we have generated using IQ test–type items could be obtained in assisted mini–learning environments for algebra, for example, one could again diagnose those ready, and those not so ready, to go beyond the level indicated by unaided static assessments of their past learning. In Vygotsky's terms, some would have a wider and some a narrower zone of proximal development. Note that zone width is not conceived of as a stable characteristic of the learner to be displayed in all domains and for all time, but rather is viewed as a fluctuating characteristic that will vary across domains and across time, and will always be, in principle, responsive to instruction. Handled with intelligence, these measures could be used in ways that would avoid the stigmatization inherent in existing static measures of general ability.

Our next steps for research, then, would be the development of adaptive testing procedures, situated in traditional academic subject domains, that would permit guided reinvention and application of knowledge. The procedures would rest heavily on detailed analyses of domain-specific knowledge, differences between novice and expert understanding, and the learning paths that traverse these developmental milestones. Advances in cognitive science and in computer technology, specifically in the fields of expert systems and intelligent tutoring systems, could marry well with these objectives.

REFERENCES

Binet, A. (1909). *Les idées modernes sur les enfants.* Paris: Ernest Flammarion.

Brown, A.L., & Campione, J.C. (1984). Three faces of transfer: Implications for early competence, individual differences, and instruction. In M. Lamb, A. Brown, & B. Rogoff (Eds.), *Advances in developmental psychology* (Vol. 3, pp. 143–192). Hillsdale, NJ: Erlbaum.

Campione, J.C., & Brown, A.L. (1984). Learning ability and transfer propensity as sources of individual differences in intelligence. In P.H. Brooks, C. McCauley, & R. Sperber (Eds.), *Learning and cognition in the mentally retarded* (pp. 265–294). Hillsdale, NJ: Erlbaum.

Vygotsky, L.S. (1978). *Mind in society: The development of higher psychological processes* (M. Cole, V. John-Steiner, S. Scribner, & E. Souberman, Eds.). Cambridge, MA: Harvard University Press.

Woodrow, H. (1917a). Practice and transference in normal and feeble-minded children: 1. Practice. *Journal of Educational Psychology, 8,* 85–96.

Woodrow, H. (1917b). Practice and transference in normal and feeble-minded children: 2. Transference. *Journal of Educational Psychology, 8,* 151–165.

Woodrow, H. (1938a). The relation between abilities and improvement with practice. *Journal of Educational Psychology, 29,* 215–230.

Woodrow, H. (1938b). The effect of practice on groups of different initial ability. *Journal of Educational Psychology, 29,* 268–278.

Woodrow, H. (1946). The ability to learn. *Psychological Review, 53,* 147–158.

7.

Intelligent Action, Learning, and Cognitive Development Might All Be Explained with the Same Theory

Earl C. Butterfield

University of Washington

Every intelligent system adds to its own fund of knowledge and repertoire of skills. All intelligent systems learn, and more intelligent systems learn more. The idea that learning increases with intelligence was advanced in the 1921 version of this monograph, but subsequent tests of the idea led to its rejection (Woodrow, 1946). Learning has not been shown to increase with intelligence, but it does not follow that intelligence and learning are unrelated. Instead, studies that failed to observe such a relationship could have been flawed, as indeed they were (Campione, Brown, & Ferrara, 1982). Learning was studied using unstructured materials, arbitrary associations, measures of rate rather than amount or kind of learning, and no teaching beyond indications of correctness. The challenge remains to determine how learning is related to intelligence.

This challenge will be easier to meet if we adopt a conception of intelligence that highlights mechanisms by which new knowledge and skills are acquired.[1] Sternberg (1985) included acquisition "components" in his theory of intelligence, but his approach is ad hoc. It asserts that intelligent humans add to their knowledge and skills, but it does not specify mechanisms of acquisition nor their relations to other mechanisms of the cog-

---

[1]The alternative approach of incorporating cognitive mechanisms into theories of learning seems unlikely to succeed, because the pretheoretical ideas of learning theory are inconsistent with the assumptions of cognitive theory (Lachman, Lachman, & Butterfield, 1979).

nitive system. A more coherent and parsimonious approach would make the acquisition of new knowledge and skills an incidental consequence of particular cognitive processes, much as memory derives from any of several cognitive activities.

The literature on cognitive differences among people identifies four factors that vary with age and intelligence and whose use might produce learning. Younger and less intelligent people have been said to have smaller and less elaborately organized knowledge bases (Butterfield, Nielsen, Tangen, & Richardson, 1985; Chi, 1981; Holzman, Pellegrino, & Glaser, 1983); to use fewer, simpler, and more passive processing strategies (Belmont & Butterfield, 1969; Brown, Campione, Bray, & Wilcox, 1973; Flavell, 1970); to have less metacognitive understanding of their own cognitive systems and of how the functioning of these systems depends upon the environment (Brown, 1978; Flavell & Wellman, 1977); and to use less complete and flexible executive processes for controlling their thinking (Butterfield & Belmont, 1977; Campione et al., 1982). When trying to account for intelligent behavior, different investigators have emphasized the importance of different ones of these four factors.[2] The few authors who have considered the role of such factors in learning also have emphasized one factor at the expense of others. Thus, Campione et al. (1982) hypothesized that executive processes are responsible for learning.

The present need is for a hypothesis about how these four factors combine to produce intelligent action and how they produce learning. One such hypothesis is that intelligent action results when "executive routines draw on base knowledge and metacognitive understandings to fashion strategies to solve current problems. Moreover, when applied to a difficult and novel problem, the same executive routines that allow current problem solution also enlarge one's base knowledge or change its representation, delete, modify, or add strategies to one's repertoire, and create new metacognitive understandings, thereby increasing one's potential for intelligent action" (Butterfield & Ferretti, in press). Executive routines include such superordinate functions as (a) setting goals in terms of responses that might solve a problem; (b) selecting from known or newly designed strategies one that is likely to lead to the goal; (c) managing implementation of the selected strategy; and (d) assessing the response resulting from the implemented strategy (Butterfield, 1981). Even though the foregoing hypothesis makes executive routines central to both intelligent action and learning, it also implies that intelligent action and learning both depend as well upon base knowledge, metacognitive understandings, and strategies. Thus, if a person understands (metacognitively) that he has solved a problem many

---

[2]Processing efficiency has been related to intelligence, but it is unclear how greater efficiency would increase learning, except indirectly by increasing time available for processes that do increase learning.

times before, he can set a goal simply by interrogating his memory (base knowledge) without (executive) recourse to analogical thinking from knowledge of similar problems. Similarly, if one understands that he has never encountered a particular problem before, he will know that he cannot retrieve an intact strategy from his base knowledge, but rather must fashion a new strategy by combining separate tactics or by analogical reasoning from strategies known to be effective for similar problems.[3]

An opportunity to learn exists whenever a person faces a problem for which he or she does not already have an effective strategy. The opportunity might be as simple as the chance to learn that a strategy already acquired for the solution of another problem will work for a new problem, in which case the lesson is a metacognitive understanding; namely, "strategy X works in this new situation as well as in the situation for which I already use it." Such learning would result if an individual's executive routines (a) recognized from his or her metacognitive understanding that the current problem is novel but similar to ones solved before; (b) called up from base knowledge a strategy that worked for similar problems; (c) tried it with the novel problem; and (d) noted that the old strategy solved the new problem.

The stage is set for the kind of learning called intellectual development whenever a problem for which one does not already know a solution is presented and that problem is one whose solution typically is acquired at a later age. Suppose that a child has strategies (a) for assessing the number of weights on each side of a tetterboard's fulcrum and (b) for assessing the distance of those weights from the fulcrum. Suppose in addition that the child knows that (c) when distances from the fulcrum are equal, the side of the tetterboard with more weights will go down; and (d) when weights are equal, the side with the weights farther from the fulcrum will go down; but suppose also that when one side has more distance and the other more weight, the child does not know how to integrate distance and weight so as to predict what the teeter-totter will do. If the child used executively guided experimentation to determine how much movement of weight equaled the addition of a weight, the child could discover either a weighted-adding or a torque-calculation strategy for solving teeter-totter problems in which weight and distance information conflict. Since both of these strategies are developmentally more advanced than is use of the base knowledge supposed for this child (Ferretti, Butterfield, Cahn, & Kerkman, 1985), such learning would be an example of executive routines promoting intellectual development.

According to the hypothesis advanced above, individual differences in

---

[3]Butterfield and Ferretti (in press) give more complete examples of how understanding, strategies, knowledge, and executive routines combine to produce intelligent action, learning, and cognitive development.

base knowledge, strategies, metacognitive understandings, and executive processes should all contribute to individual differences in intelligent action. Also, the extent and quality of a person's base knowledge and strategies should be correlated with the extent and quality of his or her metacognitive understandings and executive routines. Although definitive analyses have not been done, presently used tests of intelligence can be assumed to measure base knowledge and cognitive strategies reliably and validly. Although they do not measure metacognitive and executive processes directly, they can be assumed to measure them indirectly. It follows that it should be exceptionally difficult to increase the validity of present intelligence tests by modifying them according to the present hypothesis. Improving the tests will require a fuller view than we now possess of the independent and interactive contributions of metacognitive understandings and executive processes to intelligent action and the acquisition of new knowledge. Since only justification for changing intelligence tests should be to increase their educational and clinical utility, the view advanced here offers no reason to change the tests now.

There are several important next steps for researchers concerned with intelligence. A first one is to determine more precisely how base knowledge, metacognitive understanding, strategies, and executive routines combine to produce intelligent action. The challenge is to abandon the simplistic view that any one of these factors alone can account for any intelligent action (Chi, 1981; Keil, 1981) and to chart the various contributions of the four factors under different conditions. A second important step is to determine the conditions under which the use of executive routines leads to the solution of previously unsolvable problems. The challenge is to assess the discrepancy between people's current status on each of the four factors and the status required by a given problem, and then to determine what sorts of discrepancies lead to the greatest learning and development. A third important step is to create instructional routines from our understanding of the processes that underlie both intelligence and learning. The challenge is to move beyond the view that more intelligent people benefit from less complete instruction (Campione et al., 1982) by specifying the processes that underlie this fact. Then we will be able to build instructions that influence those processes more or less completely, depending upon the intelligence of the pupil. According to the hypothesis advanced above, intelligent action can be increased by instruction of base knowledge and strategies, but influencing subsequent learning would require the teaching of metacognitive understanding and executive routines as well. More detailed versions of such hypotheses need to be tested.

REFERENCES

Belmont, J.M., & Butterfield, E.C. (1969). The relations of short-term memory to development and intelligence. In L.P. Lipsitt & H.W. Reese (Eds.), *Advances in child development and behavior* (Vol. 4, pp. 29–82). New York: Academic Press.

Brown, A.L. (1978). Knowing when, where, and how to remember: A problem in metacognition. In R. Glaser (Ed.), *Advances in instructional psychology* Hillsdale, NJ: Erlbaum.

Brown, A.L., Campione, J.C., Bray, N.W., & Wilcox, B.L. (1973). Keeping track of changing variables: Effects of rehearsal training and rehearsal prevention in normal and retarded adolescents. *Journal of Experimental Psychology, 101,* 123–131.

Butterfield, E.C. (1981). Instructional techniques that produce generalized improvements in cognition. In P.E. Mittler (Ed.), *Frontiers of knowledge in mental retardation: Proceedings of the 5th Congress of IASSMD,* (Vol. 1, pp. 79–89). Baltimore, MD: University Park Press.

Butterfield, E.C., & Belmont, J.M. (1977). Assessing and improving the cognition of mentally retarded people. In I. Bialer & M. Sternlicht (Eds.), *Psychology of mental retardation: Issues and approaches* (pp. 277–318). New York: Psychological Dimensions.

Butterfield, E.C., & Ferretti, R.P. (in press). Toward a theoretical integration of cognitive hypotheses about intellectual differences among children. In J.G. Borkowski & J.D. Day (Eds.), *Memory and cognition in special children.* Norwood, NJ: Ablex.

Butterfield, E.C., Nielsen, D., Tangen, K.L., & Richardson, M.B. (1985). Theoretically based psychometric measures of inductive reasoning. In S. Embretson (Ed.), *Test design: Contributions from psychology, education, and psychometrics* (pp. 77–147). New York: Academic Press.

Campione, J.C., Brown, A.L., & Ferrara, R.A. (1982). Mental retardation and intelligence. In R.J. Sternberg (Ed.), *Handbook of human intelligence* (pp. 392–492). Cambridge, England: Cambridge University Press.

Chi, M.T.H. (1981). Knowledge development and memory performance. In M. Friedman, J.P. Das, & N. O'Connor (Eds.), *Intelligence and learning* (pp. 221–230). New York: Plenum.

Feretti, R.P., Butterfield, E.C., Cahn, A., & Kerkman, D. (1985). The classification of children's knowledge: Development on the balance-scale and inclined-plane tasks. *Journal of Experimental Child Psychology, 39,* 131–160.

Flavell, J.H. (1970). Developmental studies of mediated memory. In H.W. Reese & L.P. Lipsitt (Eds.), *Advances in child development and behavior* (Vol. 5, pp. 182–213). New York: Academic Press.

Flavell, J.H., & Wellman, H.M. (1977). Metamemory. In R.V. Kail & J.W. Hagen (Eds.), *Perspectives on the development of memory and cognition.* Hillsdale, NJ: Erlbaum.

Holzman, T.G., Pellegrino, J.W., & Glaser, R. (1983). Cognitive variables in series completion. *Journal of Educational Psychology, 75,* 603–618.

Keil, F.C. (1981). Constraints on knowledge and cognitive development. *Psychological Review, 88,* 197–227.

Lachman, R., Lachman, J., & Butterfield, E. (1979). *Cognitive psychology and information processing: An introduction.* Hillsdale, NJ: Erlbaum.

Sternberg, R.J. (1985). *Beyond IQ: A triarchic theory of human intelligence.* New York: Cambridge University Press.

Woodrow, H.A. (1946). The ability to learn. *Psychological Review, 53,* 147–158.

8.

What Is Intelligence?

John B. Carroll
University of North Carolina at Chapel Hill

First of all, "intelligence" must be considered as a *concept* in the mind of a society at large. All Westernized societies have this term or its approximate translation in their languages, and even in less advanced cultures, there has usually been something analogous—the equivalent, say, of what we call "shrewdness," "sagacity," or "astuteness." I shall speak, however, of the concept as it exists in societies such as ours. It embraces at least three domains of individuals' apparent competence in dealing with various situations and tasks. The society recognizes that all people have problems, and that they seem to be differentially able, other things being equal, to meet and solve those problems as they see them. The society also recognizes that problems people face are of different sorts, and of different degrees of difficulty. It is also recognized that children show increasing ability to confront problems as they grow older, but that they differ in the rate at which they approach some upper boundary of ability.

From the standpoint of the community, problems are classified into several domains: (a) academic and technical; (b) practical; and (c) social. Academic and technical problems are those arising in schoolwork, and later, in many fields of science, the professions, and occupational specialties. Practical problems are those arising in managing one's daily affairs, making a living, and planning one's course of action—even planning one's life work. Social problems are those encountered in interacting with others—individuals, groups, or even alien cultures. Thus, one can describe different kinds of intelligence: academic, practical, and social, in terms of the kinds of problems people deal with and the extent to which they appear to be able to deal with them successfully—whether for good or less desirable ends.

51

The societal concept of intelligence contains the assumption that what makes people able to deal with various kinds of problems is their ability to think about them—to consider different alternative courses of action, to create strategies of solution, and to predict consequences. It is not their *physical* capacities to act or perform that are critical, nor their *motivation,* but their *cognitive* capacities—as applied either consciously and deliberately, or unconsciously.

Further, the societal concept of intelligence contains the notion that speed of performance is at least sometimes important. It is recognized (at least in most advanced societies) that time for solving problems is not infinite, and the person who can solve a problem more quickly than another is regarded more highly, and thus possibly as more capable and "intelligent."

To a large extent, the *scientific* concept of intelligence takes off from the societal concept, or rather from the *several* concepts of intelligence held by the community at large. At least since the time of Galton, scientists have been attempting to characterize and measure different forms of intelligence. Much of the scientific work on intelligence has involved analyses of performance on what have been called psychological tests, but the study of intelligence can also involve observations of performances in learning (in school, in the psychological laboratory, and elsewhere), in the solving of "real-life" problems, and in social interaction. This work can be viewed as an attempt to bring under scientific scrutiny the concepts of intelligence held by the society—to develop more precise information about the forms of intelligence, the ways in which they are related, and the means by which they can be measured.

Science has been most successful in the analysis of academic and technical intelligence, but its findings also pertain to many aspects of practical and social intelligence. Psychological tests have been devised to sample the kinds of problems and tasks encountered in schoolwork and in those situations, occupations, and professions that involve reasoning, manipulation of mental representations, and general knowledge and use of the several symbolic systems useful in an advanced culture, principally language and mathematics. A major tool of the scientist has been factor analysis—a technique for disclosing the underlying dimensions of the abilities revealed in psychological tests, and the "structure" of these dimensions. Out of this work there have emerged several theories of the structure of abilities, ranging from a theory that emphasizes the importance of a single factor of intelligence to a theory that favors the existence of many types of ability—largely unrelated. After a thorough consideration of the various theories, the evidence for them, and the soundness of their mathematical underpinnings, I am convinced that the most acceptable and valid theory is one that posits the existence of a relatively small number of significant abilities, perhaps no more than two or three dozen—abilities that differ markedly, however, in their degree of generality, that is, the degree to which they apply to diverse kinds of tasks and performances.

The evidence is very strong that there is a "general" factor of intelligence that is involved in a great variety of cognitive tasks. It is probable that this is the same factor that Charles Spearman called g, and it is difficult to go very far beyond Spearman in his elucidation of the fundamental nature of this factor as involving what he called the "eduction of correlates and relations." Whenever a task requires noticing similarities and differences among elements, inferring correspondences, rules, and generalities, following a line of reasoning, and predicting consequences, that task is likely to involve this general factor of intelligence—particularly as the elements of the task become more numerous and complex. It seems obvious that not only many kinds of tasks on psychological tests, but also many of the academic, technical, practical, and social problems of real life involve the application of this kind of intelligence.

Not all the evidence is yet in hand, but it is likely that the general factor is identical, similar, or closely related to what R. B. Cattell has called "fluid intelligence." Possession of sufficient amounts of this general, "fluid" intelligence is also, I believe, what makes it possible for a person to acquire corresponding amounts of ability with language, mathematics, and other symbolic systems. But such attainments are only possible with sufficient exposure to these symbolic systems—through education, training, and general experience. The degree to which the individual has profited from such exposure is a measure of what Cattell has called "crystallized" intelligence.

Thus, in varying amounts, performances on a very wide variety of tasks and problems reflect abilities in general, "fluid," and "crystallized" intelligence. But depending on the nature of the task, performances also reflect degrees of ability in a number of narrower, more specialized traits, such as verbal, reasoning, numerical, perceptual speed, spatial, memory, and creative fluency abilities. Some of these more specialized abilities probably reflect mainly the degree to which the individual has learned or practiced the performances involved, but others, such as spatial ability, may chiefly reflect more fundamental, genetically conditioned traits. Expatiating on the details of our knowledge of specialized abilities is not possible here. All of these abilities, however, may be considered to be embraced, perhaps in different degrees, in a concept of intelligence.

Psychologists have sometimes been accused of "reifying" the concept of intelligence or ability. Because it can be shown, however, that there are systematic relations between individuals' characteristics and the types and difficulties of the tasks they are likely to be able to perform, there is no more reification involved than there is when a physicist infers a gravitational constant from observations of the speed of falling bodies.

In planning further steps in research on cognitive abilities, I would call for more exact knowledge of the dimensions of ability and the ways in which abilities interact with task performances of all sorts. There is also need for more knowledge about the ways in which abilities mature and change over the life span, and the extent to which they can be improved, through appropriate interventions, despite possibly being limited by inborn characteristics.

9.

On Definition of Intelligence

J. P. Das

**University of Alberta
Edmonton, Canada**

Intelligence, as the sum total of all cognitive processes, entails planning, coding of information, and attention arousal. Of these, the cognitive processes required for planning have a relatively higher status in intelligence. Planning is a broad term which includes, among other things, the generation of plans and strategies, selection from among available plans, and the execution of plans. Within the connotation of planning I include decision making. The structural base for planning is the frontal lobes, which "regulate the active state of the organism, control the essential elements of the subject's intentions, programme complex forms of activity and constantly monitor all aspects of activity" (Hecaen & Albert, 1978, p. 376).

The other two cognitive processes (coding and attention arousal), like planning, are suggested in Luria's (1966) neuropsychological work. Coding refers to two modes of processing information, simultaneous and successive. Information arriving in discrete units may be processed simultaneously or successively. The former entails the arrangement of information in a simultaneous quasi-spatial array so that the relationship between the discrete pieces of information is surveyable. An example of such processing is seen in copying a familiar drawing, such as a cube. In successive processing, the discrete information is arranged in a sequence or order; it is essentially a temporal order. Appreciation of syntax is a good example of successive processing, as is also the memory for the order in which a list of words or pictures was presented. The structural base for both processes is the posterior part of the human brain, including the occipital, parietal, and fronto-temporal areas.

The remaining process (attention arousal) is a function basic to all other higher cognitive activities. An adequate level of arousal and attention is a prerequisite for coding and planning. The function is located in the brain stem, particularly in the reticular activating system and in other structures which control attention.

The relationship between the three processes is dynamic and complex. Planning can proceed with coded information, but plans are needed to code information. Without coding, planning is empty, and without plans, coding of information is done blindly. Plans and goals help the individual in mobilizing attentional resources for a purpose. Selective and sustained attention operates throughout coding.

The three cognitive processes which underlie intelligent behavior can be identified by means of objective tests. These tests involve perception and memory, as well as higher-order symbolic operations. They also include verbal and nonverbal items, and are spread over sensory modalities. Within each of the three cognitive processes, a specific number of subprocesses can be delineated; these are based on current psychological research. The previously mentioned view of intelligence as a tripartite process does not assume one general ability. The emphasis, instead, is on processing, and on the measurement of individual and group differences in processing. The approach leads to the diagnosis of deficits in processing and to the possibilities for remediation.

What are the next most crucial steps? Until now, intelligence tests have not included measures of several important characteristics found in an intelligent person. The gifts for music, chess, and mathematics are not even measured in a preliminary manner. Other characteristics such as unusually developed social and interpersonal skills can and should be measured. Research into developing appropriate tasks to test them is worth pursuing.

However, there are other aspects of human behavior which make a person outstanding, and I am not sure if these can be gauged within the constraints of a test. I refer to those characteristics which are shared by truly great men and women. A short list of these qualities includes passion, pity, and curiosity. Fervent involvement in a cause or activity, compassion, and sustained curiosity may be easy to observe, but difficult to measure. Prolonged monitoring of a person's behavior, rather than the sampling of responses to contrived questions, is required in order to estimate such characteristics. In the model of intelligence I have proposed, these characteristics *may be* subsumed in planning, which continuously interacts with arousal (affect) and coding.

REFERENCES

Hecaen, H., & Albert, M. (1978). *Human neuropsychology.* New York: Wiley.
Luria, A.R. (1966). *Human brain and psychological processes.* New York: Harper & Row.

10.

Human Intelligence Is a Complex System of Separate Processes

Douglas K. Detterman

Case Western Reserve University

If the goal of defining intelligence is to develop a simple, empirical definition, then there can be no argument: Intelligence is that set of measures which predicts academic achievement. Indeed, IQ correlates with the number of years of education completed in adult groups about .70. This is only a variety of Boring's less specific dictum that intelligence is what intelligence tests measure.

Although this functional definition is perfectly satisfactory, it leaves nearly everybody longing for a more complete explanation of the empirical relationships it expresses. What we long for is a potential explanation of why a test score obtained in an hour's time should predict a significant aspect of a person's life. Any satisfying explanatory definition must be based on theoretical preference, of course.

In my opinion, intelligence can best be defined as a finite set of independent abilities operating as a complex system. I have made this argument before (Detterman, 1982, 1984a, 1984b), using a somewhat different approach from the one I will use here. Before presenting this argument, it is necessary to be more specific about this definition.

The purpose of this definition is to explain g, Spearman's general intellectual ability. If a battery of mental tests is subjected to factor analysis, the unrotated, first principal component defines g. This factor will account for 40–80% of the total variance in the battery. It is the g factor which seems most important in determining the power of mental tests (Jensen, 1985). It is g which must be understood if we are to understand what intelligence is.

57

It should be fairly obvious that there is a contradiction here. I have defined intelligence as a set of separate, independent processes, and yet I am claiming that these independent processes will explain a single factor, g. How is this possible? To clarify how this is not only possible, but likely, I will employ an analogy.

The analogy I will use is a university. There are several reasons that I believe this represents a good analogy for human mental ability. First, it is a complex system organized to satisfy a number of goals simultaneously. Second, structural characteristics of a university are more obvious than other complex systems which might be used as analogies. Third, and finally, since the purposes of a university include serving as a repository for old knowledge and producing new knowledge, it seems a better analogy of mental ability than are computers, factories, or machines.

In the following discussion, it should be remembered that I will not be discussing how a university operates. The important dimension will be differences between universities. What makes one university better than another? As intelligence characterizes differences between people, so I will be interested in characterizing differences between universities.

This interest in differences is an important point. It might be possible to characterize how the typical university operates, and yet know nothing about how universities differ, one from another. Similarly, we could describe general laws of mental functioning without knowing anything about what makes people different. Models of typicality may or may not be related to models of differences. However, any complete model must specify how differences arise.

It is a relatively simple matter to characterize the quality of universities. In fact, it is done all of the time. These global ratings may be on a subjective basis like experts' average ratings of quality. Or a global rating may be on an objective basis, such as the mean ranking of library size, endowment, student SAT scores, and so on. What characterizes these ratings of quality is that they are global, complex, and that they result in an index, usually consisting of a single number that ranks universities from best to worst.

Such indices of university quality are useful for many purposes. They guide students' decisions about which university to attend. They provide information to faculty and administrators about the perceived effectiveness of their programs. And they give parents a basis for justifying the cost-effectiveness of their children's decisions about what university to attend. To be useful for all of these purposes, the indices used must be generally regarded as reasonably reliable and valid. While there may be disagreements about two closely ranked schools, better schools are clearly differentiated from those that are not so good.

There are a number of things that a general index of university quality does not do. It does not provide much information about what aspects of a university should be changed to improve quality. It does not indicate which aspects of a particular university are weak and which are strong. Different universities may achieve roughly the same rank for markedly different reasons. In fact, global rankings tell us very little about the processes which produce differences in quality.

I contend that an IQ score is equivalent to global ratings of universities. It can be subjective, as in teacher ratings, or objectively based on a composite, as in an IQ score derived from the subtests of the Wechsler Adult Intelligence Scale. An IQ score is useful in making general decisions but there is a great deal that it does not do. Like global ratings of universities, IQ scores are not very useful for prescribing constructive interventions. Nor do IQ scores indicate the processes which product the differences in the global rating.

There are many interesting similarities between IQ scores and university ratings, but one of the most important for the purposes of this discussion is that both are based on complex measures of system functioning. By complex measure, I mean one that is importantly dependent on many more basic processes which are part of the system. For example, library size is a complex measure because it depends on many parts of the system. Size of endowment, demand of faculty for books and periodicals, quality of the library staff, support of alumni, commitment of the administration, availability of foundation support, age of the university, and administrative structure are just a few of the variables which might all contribute to library size.

In a similar way, performance of a complex mental ability such as is measured by a vocabulary test could be dependent on more basic processes like attention, memory, perceptual skills, and amount of reading done. The important point is that even though it is possible to characterize a system with a global index, the ability to do so says nothing about the underlying structure of the parts of the system. No one would believe that because a university ranked high on some index of quality, it therefore had more of some substance called "quality" than another university that was not so highly ranked. It would simply be concluded that the better university was doing more things right than the poorer university. However, differences in global ratings of mental ability are frequently attributed to a single characteristic of the system such as speed, fidelity, or metacomponents like strategy use.

What is it that global measures reflect, and why do they work? According to the arguments advanced above, global ratings of universities depend on complex measures which actually reflect many simpler processes of system functioning. It might be expected that the best index would be one that was an average of a number of complex measures and, in fact, this is just the sort of index that is most popular. Thus, such an index simply characterizes the average efficiency of the basic, theoretically independent subprocesses which contribute to the operation of the system. Complex measures are actually surrogate measures of many more basic processes. When the average of a diverse set of complex measures is taken, not only are surrogates for more basic processes obtained but, by averaging, a rough estimate of the extent to which each of these subprocesses is important to total system functioning is obtained. This is why several averaged complex measures are likely to work better than one as a global index of system efficiency.

By definition, a system is composed of interrelated parts. In systems theory, the degree of interrelationship is termed the "wholeness" of the system. If the operation of every part of a system is related to every other part, wholeness is said to be high. And in fact, an outcome measure taken from any part of such a system will represent the effectiveness of every part of the system to the extent that other parts enter into the outcome. Because all parts are interrelated, all of the outcome measures taken from this system will be complex measures reflecting the operation of every other part of the system and will be substantially intercorrelated.

For logical purposes, it is useful to contrast a system of high wholeness to a nonsystem in which no parts are interrelated. Measures of outcome would not reflect the operation of other parts measured and would not be intercorrelated. This is so obvious that it seems silly. But the converse, stated above, is not so easily grasped: Outcome measures from different parts of a system are correlated because those outcomes are jointly determined by common parts of the system.

What I hope is obvious is that the parts of the system themselves are interrelated but are theoretically independent in their unique operation. The only way to demonstrate this independence is to obtain less complex measures of outcome of that particular part of the system which are free of the effects of other parts of the system. As an example, it was stated above that quality of the library staff would be one variable contributing to library size. A test of librarianship skills could be devised and administered to the library staff. It would certainly be expected that the results of this test would be less correlated with university quality than would be library size. That is, the more molecular the measure, the less intimately it would be expected to be related to global indices of system functioning. However, more molecular measures would give more specific information about system functioning.

I believe the same holds true for mental ability. Certainly the human mind is a well-integrated system having a high degree of wholeness. Wholeness is reflected in complex measures of human ability, which explains the high correlations between standard tests of intelligence. Simpler, more molecular measures should be individually less highly correlated with more complex measures but should provide more specific information about the operation of the system. In fact, basic cognitive tasks correlate about .30, on the average, with more complex measures of mental ability. Whether basic cognitive tasks provide more specific information about mental abilities is yet to be determined.

In summary, I have defined human intelligence as a set of separate basic abilities enmeshed in a complex system of relationships. The relationships between various measures of this system are no different from what we should expect to find in any well-integrated system. Success in understanding this system of mental abilities will be a direct function of our ability to obtain independent measures of the various parts of the system.

The implications of this position for both research and future test development are clear. To obtain a better understanding of mental ability we must develop more precise, more molecular measures of the separate parts of the system. A natural result of this research will be tests which provide more specific information about mental functioning and which should be far more useful in planning interventions.

REFERENCES

Detterman, D.K.(1982). Does "g" exist? *Intelligence, 6,* 99–108.

Detterman, D.K. (1984a). Understand cognitive components before postulating metacomponents, etc, part 2. *Behavioral and Brain Sciences, 7,* 289–290.

Detterman, D.K. (1984b). g-Whiz: Review of H.J. Eysenk (Ed.), *A Model for Intelligence. Contemporary Psychology, 29,* 375–376.

Jensen, A.R. (1985, April). *The g beyond factor analysis.* Paper presented in Buros-Nebraska Symposium on Measurement and Testing, University of Nebraska, Lincoln, NE.

11.

Where Is Intelligence?

W. K. Estes
Harvard University

The question "What is intelligence?" seems unlikely to be resolved with much broader agreement in 1986 than it was in a similar symposium 60-odd years ago (*Journal of Educational Psychology,* 1921). But sometimes reframing a refractory question leads to some advance. The considerations leading to my rephrasing will shortly become evident.

The elusive concept of intelligence. There is a very large literature on intelligence, but it is curiously constrained to treatment as a special topic within psychology. One might, on rational a priori grounds, expect to find intelligence to be a ubiquitous entry in texts on cognitive processes, but, in fact, one can scan through the tables of contents of all such volumes on a typical library shelf (e.g., Anderson, 1980; Bourne, Dominowksi, & Loftus, 1979; Glass, Holyoak, & Santa, 1979; Lindsay & Norman, 1972; Solso, 1979; Wickelgren, 1979) without finding one occurrence of the term. Neither does one find an entry for intelligence in the widespread information-flow diagrams of the cognitive system. Thus, in either sense of the question "Where is intelligence?" in cognition and cognitive psychology, the answer would seen to be either "Nowhere" or "Everywhere." Which is correct may depend on how deeply one looks.

The grip of tradition. The view of intelligence as a measurable trait or aspect of the individual seems to have changed little in either content or breadth of acceptance from the time of Binet to the present. And this continuity clearly is largely attributable to an impressive record of success

Preparation of this chapter was supported in part by Grant BNS 80–26656 from the National Science Foundation.

at predicting variation in task performance (in schools or in activities depending strongly on schooling) from tests labeled as intelligence scales. One sees increasingly frequent attempts at rebellion against the psychometric tradition (Carroll, 1982; Resnick, 1976; Sternberg & Detterman, 1979), but with limited effects on prevailing viewpoints and practices. A basic problem is that the development of theory about human intelligence is caught in a loop. We see increasing success at obtaining theoretically meaningful measures of cognitive abilities in well-analyzed laboratory tasks (Hunt, 1978), but evidence of relevance to the concept of intelligence comes mainly from correlations of new measures with scores on ability tests whose validity, in turn, depends on correlations with the criteria of the psychometric tradition. Is there any way out of the loop?

Human and machine intelligence. If there is a way out, finding it may depend on some fairly radical reorientation. And since a constructive reorientation does not seem to be forthcoming from within psychology, perhaps we need to look elsewhere. A direction that strikes me as potentially fruitful points toward artificial intelligence, another discipline concerned with theoretical problems of intelligence but deriving from a very different intellectual tradition. Whereas the psychologist starts from the premise that intelligence exists as an attribute of the human mind and tries to define and measure it in situ, investigators starting from a base in computer science assume only that intelligence characterizes all information processors, animate or inanimate, that can perform intellectual tasks. These investigators propose to test the validity of their ideas by actually constructing intelligent systems.

How does one decide whether a machine is intelligent, or that one machine is more intelligent than another? Consideration of the tasks that can be accomplished is one factor, but, in contrast to the situation with human intelligence, only an auxiliary one. By and large, a machine that can play chess will be regarded as more intelligent than one that can only play tic-tac-toe. But even a machine that can defeat a master chess player will not be considered very intelligent if its strategy is limited to following out search trees of possible sequences of moves mechanically. Similarly, a machine that behaves as though it understands natural language in some domain is not credited with much intelligence if it has all relevant sentences stored in memory together with response instructions and simply goes through a lookup procedure when given an input. In each case, the machine is credited with intelligence only to the extent that it carries out the task in an intelligent way—"intelligent way" being defined in theoretical terms.

The rapid development of the field of artificial intelligence over the past 25 years has not brought us close to a satisfactory general theory of intelligent function, but there is substantial agreement at least on some constituents (see, for example, Hunt, 1975; Newell & Simon, 1981). One of these is a capacity for symbol manipulation, perhaps the most basic property of intelligent systems. A second is a capacity for evaluating the consequences of alternative choices (as the alternative moves available at a given point in a chess game) without following out all resulting sequences to their conclusions. A third is the property that searches over sequences of symbols (moves in a game, items in a search for a vocabulary item, branches of the decision tree of a classification task) be guided by knowledge and heuristic principles.

There is a sharp contrast between the role of knowledge in the psychometric and in the computational approaches to intelligence. In the former, knowledge of facts or word meanings is considered to be an index of intelligence (and therefore a suitable ingredient of tests). In the latter, knowledge is now regarded as an essential ingredient of intelligence, not simply a correlate of some more abstract characteristic. Although this latter view is not often expressed in the psychological literature on intelligence, it does reflect some current thinking about the evolution of intelligent function and its variation with phylogenetic level.

> Perhaps the most striking distinction between human and animal learning has to do with the time scale of the acquisition and use of information. In animals, learning mainly has to do with information relevant to their current problems, though there are some exceptions (for example, acquiring information about broad features of an environmental locale or territory). In human learning, it is the rule rather than the exception for information acquisition to have little to do with current problems or tasks. Sometimes a long-term purpose for information being acquired is discernible, but sometimes information appears to be gathered and stored in memory for its own sake. (Estes, 1984, p. 620)

In that last sentence, we might well replace "for its own sake" with "as an integral part of the process of developing intelligence."

It is by no means the case that the reorientation toward intelligence that I have sketched derives entirely from computer science. In the early days of artificial intelligence, there was much optimism that the principles of building intelligent systems could come entirely from the sciences of computing and computability. However, the early optimism was not borne out. Many of the major advances in artificial intelligence, in areas ranging from sensory information processing to expert decision making, have been associated with two-way interactions between computational and cognitive research and the building of aspects of human mental functioning into intelligent computer systems (Cohen & Feigenbaum, 1982; Hunt, 1975). To take account of these interactions, the proposed reorientation may appropriately be termed the cognitive science perspective.

How might research and practice be influenced by this perspective? For one thing, there might be less tendency to let evaluations of research on intelligence hinge on the production of new indices that correlate highly with traditional measures. Also, the task of assessing the intelligence of a person would be less a matter of determining how many of a standardized set of tasks the person can complete than of analyzing how the tasks are accomplished and diagnosing the processes that are implicated. There have been some efforts toward this kind of analysis (for example, Cole & Scribner, 1974; Estes, 1974, 1981; Royer, 1971; Tulving, 1985), but so far they are scattered and without much cumulative impact.

Intelligence: What and Where? A flip answer to this question is "Nothing and nowhere." New advances toward the understanding of intelligence are coming from research that cuts across traditional boundaries of psychometrics, cognitive psychology, and computational science. From the cognitive science perspective, intelligence is not a trait to be measured by success rates on samples of test performance. Rather, it is a multifaceted aspect of the processes that enable animate or inanimate systems to accomplish tasks that involve information processing, problem solving, and creativity.

> It would seem, then, that progress toward untangling the multiple determinants of individual differences in intelligent behavior can come only within the framework of more comprehensive theories of the whole interactive cognitive system. (Estes, 1982, pp. 217–218)

REFERENCES

Anderson, J.R. (1980). *Cognitive psychology and its implications* San Francisco, CA: W.H. Freeman.

Bourne, L.E., Jr., Dominowski, R.L., & Loftus, E.F. (1979). *Cognitive processes* Englewood Cliffs, NJ: Prentice-Hall.

Carroll, J.B. (1982). The measurement of intelligence. In R.J. Sternberg (Ed.), *Handbook of human intelligence* (pp. 29–120). Cambridge, England: Cambridge University Press.

Cohen, P.R., & Feigenbaum, E.A. (1982). *Handbook of artificial intelligence* (Vol. 3), Los Altos, CA: William Kaufmann.

Cole, M., & Scribner, S. (1974). *Culture and thought: A psychological introduction.* New York: Wiley.

Editors. (1921). Intelligence and its measurement: A symposium [Special issue]. *Journal of Educational Psychology, 12,* 123–147, 195–216.

Estes, W.K. (1974). Learning theory and intelligence. *American Psychologist, 29,* 740–749.

Estes, W.K. (1981). Intelligence and learning. In M.P. Friedman, J.P. Das, & N. O'Connor (Eds.), *Intelligence and learning* (pp. 3–23). New York: Plenum.

Estes, W.K. (1982). Learning, memory, and intelligence. In R.J. Sternberg (Ed.), *Handbook of human intelligence* (pp. 170–224). New York: Cambridge University Press.

Estes, W.K. (1984). Human learning and memory. In P. Marler & H.S. Terrace (Eds.), *The biology of learning* (pp. 617–628). Berlin: Springer-Verlag.

Glass, A.L., Holyoak, K.J., & Santa, J.L. (1979). *Cognition.* Reading, MA: Addison-Wesley.

Hunt, E.B. (1975). *Artificial intelligence* New York: Academic Press.

Hunt, E. (1978). Mechanics of verbal ability. *Psychological Review, 85,* 109–130.

Lindsay, P.H., & Norman, D.A. (1972). *Human information processing: An introduction to psychology.* New York: Academic Press.

Newell, A., & Simon, H.A. (1981). Computer science as empirical inquiry: Symbols and search. In J. Haugeland (Ed.), *Mind design: Philosophy, psychology, artificial intelligence* (pp. 35–66). Montgomery, VT: Bradford Books.

Resnick, L.B. (Ed.). (1976). *The nature of intelligence.* Hillsdale, NJ: Erlbaum.

Royer, F.L. (1971). Information processing of visual figures in the digit symbol substitution test. *Journal of Experimental Psychology, 87,* 335–342.

Solso, R.L. (1979). *Cognitive psychology.* New York: Harcourt Brace Jovanovich.

Sternberg, R.J., & Detterman, D.K. (Eds.). (1979). *Human intelligence: Perspectives on its theory and measurement.* Norwood, NJ: Ablex.

Tulving, E. (1985). Memory and consciousness. *Canadian Psychology, 26,* 1–12.

Wickelgren, W.A. (1979). *Cognitive psychology.* Englewood Cliffs, NJ: Prentice-Hall.

12.

Is Intelligence?

Hans Eysenck
Institute of Psychiatry, London

Most efforts to study and define intelligence have adopted what Kuhn (1962) has called the "resolutive" approach, that is, they have attempted to resolve and reduce complex phenomena into elementary parts and processes. Thus intelligence was defined in terms of learning capacity, memory, problem solving ability, reasoning, judgment, adaptation to environment, comprehension, the evolvement of strategies, and many other concepts, although clearly these are all *consequences* of the application of intelligence, and therefore cannot serve as *definitions*. This was recognized by Hebb (1949) in the distinction between Intelligence A and Intelligence B, with the former denoting the organism's basic ability to do all the things enumerated above, while the latter is the level of cognitive performance actually shown by an organism in everyday life situations. Intelligence B comes closer to the layman's notion of "intelligence," but it is so complex, being not only a reflection of Intelligence A, but also powerfully influenced by factors like education, socio-economic states, personality, parental influence, nutrition, motivation, and many others, that it is not useful as a scientific concept. IQ tests of the Binet type have attempted to reduce the influence of these factors, with some success, and have usually given good predictions of success in fields where cognitive abilities are clearly required, such as education, business, the armed forces, etc. (Eysenck, 1979). Such tests represent a technology which, while successful, lacks proper scientific underpinnings. Thus the IQ is usually treated as a *unitary* variable, but has been shown to be decomposable into three independent parts— mental speed, error checking, and continuance or persistence (Eysenck, 1982; Furneaux, 1961; White, 1982).

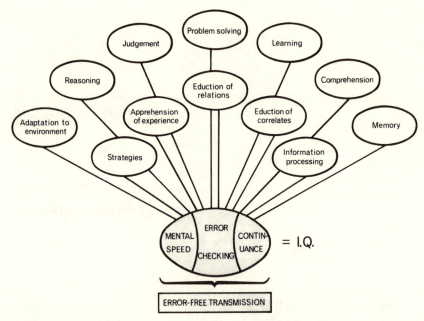

Figure 1. Relationship of Intelligence A to IQ and Intelligence B (From Eysenck, 1985).

Spearman (1927) defined the popular approach to definition by looking for empirical support for the existence of a *general factor* (*g*) of intelligence in the patterns of intercorrelations between tests of many different kinds. This furnishes us with an *explicandum,* but not with a definition. It serves to disprove Binet's notion of intelligence as nothing more than an *average* of unconnected separate cognitive abilities, and establishes that it is scientifically meaningful to postulate intelligence as a major factor in analyzing differences between people in cognitive performance.

The honor of having postulated a *causal* theory and definition of intelligence belongs to Sir Francis Galton, who looked for a *biological* source of individual differences in cognitive ability. His conceptions have recently been revived and put into testable form by two groups of workers. Jensen (1982a, b) and the members of the Erlangen School (Lehrl, 1983) have shown that Galton was right in postulating a close link between Reaction Time (RT) and intelligence. Eysenck and Barrett (1985) have summarized evidence that evoked potentials in the EEG (average evoked potential [AEP]) correlate highly with psychometric intelligence (Wechsler Adult Intelligence Scale [WAIS]), and Eysenck (1985) has brought together these various strands into a nomological network which supports a theory of intelligence as being essentially the outcome of *error-free transmission of information through the cortex.*

Figure 1 shows the assumed relationship between this fundamental property of the central nervous system (CNS), IQ as measured by traditional psychometric devices, and Intelligence B, in all its variety. Intelligence A can best be measured by direct involvement of the underlying physiological bases responsible for the creation of individual differences; this is the most fundamental and scientifically meaningful type of measure that we can make. Closely allied would be measurement of response time duration and variability, although this is already at least a step removed from the basic physiological variables in question.

Measurement of Intelligence B must involve different tests for different populations, depending on past experience, schooling, and other environmental factors. Clearly it must be based on factor-analytic information, preferring high-loading tests to low-loading tests. The content and format should be as varied as possible, to include as many aspects of intelligence as possible. Special cognitive abilities (Group factors; primary abilities) are of practical importance, but by definition orthogonal to g and hence unconnected with intelligence.

It follows naturally from this new approach that the next steps in research should (1) attempt to test the theory put forward by experimental studies of the AEP; (2) look in greater detail into the relationship between Intelligence A, so defined, and IQ (both on total score and in terms of the three aspects into which it has been divided); (3) estimate the contribution of heredity and environment to AEP scores, as opposed to IQ scores; (4) look at the growth and decline of intelligence, in neonates and the aged, by means of AEPs; and (5) assess the social importance of Intelligence A, as compared with IQ. This new approach is in essence a Kuhnian revolution, and hence calls forth an enormous amount of "normal science" effort of the puzzle-solving kind. Only along these lines will we transmogrify the technology of IQ testing into a proper natural-science type of measurement.

REFERENCES

Eysenck, H.J. (1979). *The structure and measurement of intelligence.* New York: Springer.
Eysenck, H.J. (Ed.). (1982). A model for intelligence. New York: Springer.
Eysenck, H.J. (1986). The theory of intelligence and the psychophysiology of cognition. In R.J. Sternberg (Ed.), *Advances in the psychology of human intelligence* (Vol. 3). Hillsdale, NJ: Erlbaum.
Eysenck, H.J., & Barrett, P. (1985). Psychophysiology and the measurement of intelligence. In C.R. Reynolds & V. Wilson (Eds.), *Methodological and statistical advances in the study of individual differences.* New York: Plenum.
Furneaux, W.D. (1961). Intellectual abilities and problem-solving behaviour. In H.J. Eysenck (Ed.), *Handbook of abnormal psychology* (pp. 167–192). New York: Basic Books.

Hebb, D.O. (1949). *The organization of behaviour.* New York: Wiley.

Jensen, A.R. (1982a). Reaction time and psychometric *g.* In H.J. Eysenck (Ed.), A model for intelligence (pp. 93–132). New York: Springer.

Jensen, A.R. (1982b). The chronometry of intelligence. In R.J. Sternberg (Ed.), *Advances in the psychology of human intelligence.* (Vol. 1, pp. 242–267). Hillsdale, NJ: Erlbaum.

Kuhn, T. (1962). *The structure of scientific revolutions.* Chicago: University of Chicago Press.

Lehrl, S. (1983). Intelligenz: Informationspsychologische Grundlagen. *Enzyklopädie der Naturwissenschaft und Technik.* Landsberg: Moderne Industrie.

Spearman, C. (1927). *The abilities of man.* London: Macmillan.

White, O. (1982). Some major components in general intelligence In H.J. Eysenck (Ed.), A model for intelligence (pp. 44–90). New York: Springer.

13.

The Waning of Intelligence Tests

Howard Gardner

Boston Veterans Administration Medical Center
Boston University School of Medicine
Harvard Project Zero

As a member of a Western society, I have grown up with the word *intelligence* buzzing in my ears, and intelligence tests (and their next of kin) have never been remote from my consciousness. Yet my own training in psychology did not center upon issues of intelligence, and until recently neither I nor others have viewed me as a contributor to the vast literature on intelligence and intelligence testing. I am, therefore, especially grateful to the conveners for inviting me to participate in this symposium. I am afraid, however, that I shall have to impose upon their generosity for, perhaps owing to my atypical approach to issues of intelligence, I have reservations about the way they have formulated their questions.

The concept of intelligence arose because of a perceived need to rank individuals on a dimension judged of importance for scholastic achievement; intelligence tests have emerged as a remarkably successful (though probably not essential) instrument for achieving that end in our culture. Like many successful instruments, however, intelligence tests are used because they work at their appointed task rather than because they reflect a clearly thought-through (and clearly defensible) rationale. And, again, like many other successful inventions, they have been called on to do more than they can sustain.

In approaching the area of intelligence in *Frames of Mind* (Gardner, 1983), I conducted a Gendanken experiment. First of all, I tried to erase from my mind any notion of intelligence as usually formulated (a single trait with which an individual is presumably endowed) or of intelligence tests

73

(simple short-answer, paper-and-pencil, or interview instruments which purport to reveal an individual's intellectual potential over the course of an hour or so). Then I let my imagination play over the wide range of end-states which have been valued in diverse human cultures: hunters, farmers, military leaders, civil authorities, artists, musicians, religious leaders, shamans, parents, athletes, and the like. I also picked out three test cases—a sailor in the South Seas, a student of the Koran, a composer working at a microcomputer. The challenge, as I saw it, was to evolve a view of cognition which was fully equal to accounting for and assessing the range of abilities which have been valued in diverse societies across human history.

In formulating this comprehensive view, I studied what is known about the nature and evolution of cognition in the human nervous system; I also examined evidence on how these cognitive powers have been marshaled to diverse intellectual ends. I then introduced a definition of an intelligence. As I came to formulate it, an intelligence is an ability (or skill) to solve problems or to fashion products which are valued within one or more cultural settings. It is important to note that nothing is said in this definition about the singularity (or plurality) of intelligence, about short answers or standardized tests, or about factor analysis or the prediction of scholastic accomplishment. This simple identification of what is *not* entailed in this definition highlights the numerous assumptions which creep in when we invoke the term *intelligence* in an unexamined way.

Armed with this definition, I then surveyed a wide range of criteria, ranging from the kinds of abilities found in prodigies or idiot savants, to the symptomatology exhibited by brain-damaged patients. This survey, which I candidly dubbed a subjective factor analysis, yielded seven candidate intelligences: linguistic, logical-mathematical, musical, spatial, bodily-kinesthetic, interpersonal, and intrapersonal. No claims are made about the sacrosanctity of the particular intelligences identified, the levels of analyses featured, or the *number* of intelligences nominated. Using my or other criteria, researchers are welcome to come up with their own list of intelligences. Nonetheless, the present list seems a reasonable set of candidates for accounting for the end-states valued in different cultures; by drawing on these intelligences in various ways, individuals should be able to solve problems or fashion products (and researchers should be able to model their performances).

Given such a broad-based theory, it is possible to proceed in many different ways. At present, my own interests have led me in three directions: (a) an effort, undertaken with David Feldman, to assess the intellectual propensities of young children, by devising environments in which their play (or work) with different materials will reveal particular patterns of intellectual strength and weakness; (b) an exploration, undertaken with Joseph Walters and Mara Krechevsky, of the relationship between the development of an intelligence in individuals with normal aptitude, compared with its development in individuals who exhibit special gifts early on, or who eventually attain an exceptionally high level of mastery, or even a unique degree of competence; (c) a study, conducted with the same two colleagues, of the particular developmental trajectories of an intelligence, in order to ferret out patterns which may be particular to one intelligence, as against those which characterize other intelligences. In this latter enterprise, we have been aided by classroom teachers, whose considerable knowledge about growth in various intellectual domains has been largely ignored by educational researchers.

It is evident from the foregoing that my view of intelligence and my research program is quite far afield from that described in the *Journal of Educational Psychology* 65 years ago, or in the journal *Intelligence* today. (It is correspondingly closer to the interests of many classroom teachers and school administrators.) I of course hope that such lines of work will enter the mainstream of work in intelligence, but I am not optimistic. If asked to predict, I would guess there will continue to be a search for better and more rapidly administered standardized (group) tests, which can predict more of *g* with fewer items, or, better yet, with a single neurological measure. In our technologically oriented society, such a search is likely to continue for a long time. My own guess is that such a search will prove as forlorn as the alchemical search for a fountain of youth, but I certainly would not block the road of inquiry.

My vision is quite different. I seek a better understanding of the *contents* of each intelligence—the structures and processes involved in becoming proficient in, for example, musical understanding, interpersonal sensitivity, linguistic usage, or scientific creation. I urge more attention to ecological and ethological lines of evidence: Studies of the organism embedded in its natural and cultural environment may help to identify those structures which are initially mobilized by particular objects or materials, as well as suggesting the processes of canalization or diversification which may then ensue. Those of us interested in intelligence should not shy away from the most challenging if most difficult issues: How can we conceptualize and account for wisdom, synthesizing ability, intuition, metaphoric capacities, humor, good judgment? And while recognizing that psychology is always most comfortable with performance hovering around the mean, we should seek to explain the highest levels of achievement in whatever realm they may emerge.

Marx hoped that one day the state would simply wither away, no longer needed and hardly missed. In my personal millennial vision, I imagine the apparatus of intelligence testing as eventually becoming unnecessary, its waning unmourned. An hour-long standardized test may at certain points in history have served as a reasonable way of indicating who should be performing better at school or who is capable of military service; but as we come to understand the variety of roles and the variety of ways in which scholastic or military accomplishment can come about, we need far more differentiated and far more sensitive ways of assessing what individuals are capable of accomplishing. In place of standardized tests, I hope that we can develop environments (or even societies) in which individuals' natural and acquired strengths would become manifest: environments in which their daily solutions of problems or fashioning of products would indicate clearly which vocational and avocational roles most suit them.

As we move toward constructing such environments, there will be less of a need for formal and context-free kinds of evaluations because the distance between what students are doing and what they will need (or want) to do in the society will be correspondingly narrowed. We do not have tests to determine who will become a good leader because leadership abilities emerge under naturally occurring circumstances and this kind of evidence speaks for itself. Nor do we have tests for sex appeal, football playing, musical performance, or legislative powers, for much the same reasons. We designed tests for intelligence because it did not prove easy to observe this alleged global property in the real world; but this is perhaps because intelligence as a single, measurable capacity was never well-motivated to begin with.

If the kinds of naturally occurring cognition that I have described are valid, then their several manifestations ought to be readily discernible through judicious observations in the individual's ordinary environment. Far from rendering psychologists or psychometricians unemployable, however, a shift to this kind of subtle measurement would require outstanding efforts from a much larger, more broadly trained, and more imaginative cadre of workers. When one thinks about the enormous human potential currently wasted in a society which values only a small subset of human talents, such an investment seems worthwhile.

REFERENCE

Gardner, H. (1983). *Frames of mind: The theory of multiple intelligences.* New York: Basic Books.

14.

Intelligence as Acquired Proficiency

Robert Glaser
University of Pittsburgh

Introduction: Intellectual and Athletic Proficiency

My current definition of intelligence can be introduced by noting the similarities between intellectual and athletic proficiency. Indelicate as this may sound, it's not a new comparison. In his book *Thinking, An Experimental and Social Study,* Bartlett (1958) introduced his studies by discussing the nature of "bodily skill" and the properties of skilled performance. He suggested that

> It seems reasonable to try to begin by treating thinking provisionally as a complex and high-level kind of skill. Thinking has its acknowledged experts, like every other known form of skill, and in both cases much of the expertness, though never, perhaps, all of it, has to be acquired by well-informed practice. . . .
>
> But it is extremely important to realize that the case for beginning a study of the thought processes by using as clues what is already known and established about the measurement and nature of bodily skill, does not, in any important sense, rest upon these. (pp. 11–12)

Consider, then, the nature of various athletic proficiencies. They appear to share the following characteristics:

- An available knowledge structure (schema or script) of the domain of competence (the game or skill) which is elaborated with experience.

77

- Fine-honed, automated performance components that allow precise timing and fast perceptual reactions to information.
- Chunking of discrete events into groupings and classifications that enable pattern recognition and planful sequences of actions. (As is revealed, for example, in the play of the badminton champion or baseball professional, who think in terms of sequences of actions that go beyond a particular stroke or throw.)
- Inherited physiological systems, for example, muscular development and an efficient cardiovascular system, that are further developed with appropriate exercise.
- A constancy of performance that is maintained over a long period of time, declines with disuse and with aging of the physiological system, and recovers with use. Sometimes this performance is maintained over longer periods because of the well-organized knowledge structures of experienced performers.
- A tacit understanding in experts that often makes them unable to describe the full particulars of their performances. Coaches who observe skill and its development are much better at analyzing skilled competence for the purposes of training.
- Parameters of individual differences and individual "styles" are very apparent.
- Proficiency that is specific to particular domains of performance. Although some performance components and a good physiological system contribute to "all-around ability," expertise of one kind is not necessarily transferable to other types of performance.
- Competence that can be assisted and extended by artificial aids and specially designed inventions and equipment (such as high jump poles, track shoes, and track surfaces) that are derived from study and increased understanding of performance.
- Over time, with good motivational conditions, such aids improve records of performance and foster new forms and levels of proficiency.
- At the limits of expert performance, flexibility, adaptiveness, and inventiveness allow further elaboration of knowledge and skill, especially when novel, nonstandard situations are encountered.

The above characteristics and statements seem to apply to intellectual performance as well as to athletic prowess. But it is not surprising that the phenomena apparent in one domain of human performance resemble those of other domains. These resemblances are a useful guide for considering the nature and nurture of intelligence. Conceiving of intelligence as a form of proficiency enables us to remove it from the realm of mysterious capacities and renders it trainable, amenable to external support, and open to discovery of its limits.

Intelligence as Cognitive Proficiency

My definition of intelligence follows. Intelligence is proficiency (or competence) in intellectual cognitive performance. (The word intellectual here serves to differentiate it from "emotional" cognition.) Intelligence can be low or high, awkward or graceful, narrow or broad, swiftly or more slowly acquired. Of course, this definition requires another: What is proficient intellectual performance? The answer requires a distinction (hardly mutually exclusive or noninteractive) between two categories of performance: artifactually constrained proficiency, and naturally constrained proficiency.[1]

Intelligence in artifactual domains refers to proficiency in the "invented" knowledge and skill domains of a society or culture, for example, areas of science, physics, chemistry, and economics; vocational-technical proficiencies; and other valued and transmitted domains of human knowledge and service (including certain social and personal skills typical of various cultures and subcultures.) These competencies are usually acquired under relatively formal instructional conditions in school, through formal self-instruction, through social learning and modeling in a family and community.

Intelligence in natural domains refers to pervasive competences or proficiencies that occur early in human development, for example, what Keil (1981) refers to as ontological knowledge (basic categories of existence), first language proficiency, general spatial knowledge and related perceptual abilities, knowledge of regularities such as are involved in elementary concepts of numbers, causal thinking, classification skills, and other regularities observed by the senses. Proficiency in these natural domains is broadly applicable in acquiring artifactual proficiencies. Intelligence in natural domains, like intelligence in artifactual domains, is acquired on the basis of cognitive structures and processes, but is learned more informally and spontaneously than artifactual domain intelligence. The knowledge structures and cognitive processes involved are heavily derived from naturally occurring as contrasted with culturally and socially codified events.

As a function of stage of development and situational or task requirements, both artifactually derived and natural knowledge and skill comprise forms of intellectual performance and attained cognitive proficiencies that can be called intelligence. Thus, adults, highly proficient and expert in performances required in their jobs and in life problems, display intelligence, as do children who become highly skilled in the representation of numerosity and in numerical reasoning through early categorization and

---

[1]My colleague Stellan Ohlsson points out a similar distinction between natural and technical knowledge domains (see Ohlsson, 1983).

counting skills. Such performances represent intelligence as encouraged and valued by a culture and as defined by the structure of a domain.

The domains of artifactually and naturally constrained intelligence overlap and interact as a function of the tasks and environmental situations encountered by a child or an adult. For example, number concepts and principles start out as primarily natural knowledge domains and become integrated into the artifactual domains of mathematics. Other intelligent performances like musical talent and spatial ability seem to be similarly developed. The measurable dimensions of intelligence should reflect the nature and extent of the proficiencies that are attained. (The various cognitive performances that might be assessed for this purpose are described in the last section of this essay.) The quality and degree of this attainment, as with athletic proficiency, are determined by the interactive knowledge-process properties of a domain, as acquired and elaborated by opportunities for experience, and as assisted by invented aids, cultural demands, and social motivation.

Learning and Required Research

The means and timing of acquiring cognitive proficiencies in both artifactual and natural domains influence the characteristics of intelligent performance; cognitive proficiency can be acquired in different ways and at different rates. Slower learners and fast learners can acquire similar levels of intelligence. Thus, significant questions in research on intelligence involve the nature of learning: How do artifactual and natural proficiencies interact with increasing age and experience? How do cognitive structures and processes change, and what are the constraints on these changes? What are the characteristics and properties of various levels of proficiency that define assessable levels of intelligent performance? Investigation of such questions is demanded by the definition of intelligence proposed in this essay, which centers on the quality of the cognitive proficiency attained—and bypasses the reification of a learning ability. The emphasis here on attained competence differs from definitions of intelligence that make cognitive proficiency equivalent to ability to learn.

In large measure, knowledge structures associated with domain-specific proficiency enable the cognitive processes that are critical to the acquisition of further proficiency. These processes foster the rapid access to organized memory, chunking, forms of representation, and self-regulatory skills that are required for coping with tasks and problem situations and lead to new organizations and integrations of information. Learning occurs through the utilization of such proficiencies and results in the intelligences that exist in the context of natural and artifactual domains.

The generalized cognitive processes identified by psychometric analyses, as well as the general methods and heuristic processes uncovered in cognitive studies of human problem solving on knowledge-lean tasks, appear to be involved when an individual is confronted with unfamiliar domains—domains in which specific proficiency may not have been attained. However, these general processes may be less differentiating of individual variation in cognitive proficiency than the domain-specific intelligence that is nurtured over the course of life-span development. It is also conceivable that generally applicable processes are acquired as an individual operates in a wide variety of domains, so that the common structures and processes employed become available for mapping and analogical reasoning to new domains.

Measuring Intelligence

When intelligence is considered as cognitive proficiency, the performances that index the quality and level of intelligence are similar in artifactual and natural domains, and most likely entail their integration. Recent investigations of expertise in various fields suggest general guidelines for assessing intellectual proficiency:

- Proficiency in one domain is no guarantee of proficiency in others, and forms of intellectual proficiency differ as a function of the domains in which they develop. However, competence in certain domains may be more generalizable and lead to possibilities for a wide span of intellectual proficiency. Individuals competent in a number of different domains may develop generalizable proficiencies (mapping and analogical strategies) that enable them to transfer abilities across domains.
- Intelligence is manifested by the ability to perceive large, meaningful patterns of information rapidly. (This pattern recognition occurs so rapidly that it takes on the character of the "intuitions.") Individuals with less proficiency recognize patterns that are smaller, less articulated, more literal and surface-structure oriented, and that are less derivative of inferences and higher level principles in a domain.
- Intelligence is characterized by dynamic proceduralized knowledge. Concepts and declarative knowledge are bound to procedures for their application and to conditions under which these procedures are useful.
- Intellectual proficiency facilitates representational capabilities and the perception of situations in ways that greatly reduce the role of memory search. Individuals who are less proficient in a domain display a good deal of general search and processing. Proficient individuals rely on general heuristic processes when specialized schemata are not avail-

able—particularly in unfamiliar situations or situations that test limits of their proficiency.

- Intellectual proficiency depends on the development of automaticity in basic performance processes. Automaticity frees working memory for higher level processing. High levels of competence may emerge after extended practice leading to the development of performance automaticity.

- Intelligence is limited and shaped by the task structures and environment in which it is exercised. People attempt to meet the level of competence necessary to an activity or problem. Hence, in efficiency-oriented environments, where there is repeated application with little variation, routine forms of intelligence develop.

- Analytical tasks and environments or cultures where understanding and innovation are valued along with efficient performance encourage variation and nonroutine adaptations.

- Requirements for competences that are highly flexible encourage resourcefulness in the face of new information. Given such requirements, intelligent individuals show fast access to multiple possible interpretations and representations. Such intellectual proficiency is accompanied by the development of skilled self-regulatory (metacognitive) processes, such as performance monitoring, allocation of attention, sensitivity to informational feedback, and so on. As the demands of a task or environment become more or less stable, opportunities to extend competence may be less forthcoming.

Thus, intelligence in both artifactual and natural domains is constrained by organized structures of knowledge, depends upon automated basic performance processes, engenders metacognitive self-regulatory processes, and is influenced by environmental and cultural requirements and limits. The differences between cognitive proficiencies in artifactual and natural domains are apparent in the study of formally instructed systems such as expert-novice studies, in contrast to the study of the more spontaneously acquired abilities investigated by developmental psychologists. As compared with the invented knowledge structures of artifactual domains, the structures involved in the development of natural proficiencies are available early in life, before extensive experience with artifactual domains. As the structures of formally instructed domains are introduced, they interact with natural proficiencies. Increasingly, specific manifestations of intelligence develop and the individual adapts schema-driven proficiencies in artifactual and natural domains as necessary.

The situations of everyday life and work in a culture involve the joint operation of natural and artifactual structures and, depending upon task demands, involve a shunting off to increased reliance on one or the other.

With experience, this shunting relies more on specific artifactual competence; natural competencies may be emphasized when the limits of artifactual proficiency are pushed, much as in sports when the limits of athletic competence are tested. In the future, we can anticipate that, like athletic proficiency, intellectual proficiency will continue to be enhanced by aids to human performance, and expected limits of intelligence will be exceeded.

REFERENCES

Bartlett, F. (1958). *Thinking: An experimental and social study.* New York: Basic Books.
Keil, F.C. (1981). Constraints on knowledge and cognitive development. *Psychological Review, 88* (3), 204–205.
Ohlsson, S. (1983). On natural and technical knowledge domains. *Scandinavian Journal of Psychology, 24,* 89–91.

15.

A Social View of Intelligence

Jacqueline J. Goodnow

Macquarie University
Sydney, Australia

We have been asked three questions: What is intelligence? What are the pressing research topics? And what implications do our answers have for the nature of testing? My replies are mainly in the form of arguments for research on three topics: (a) intelligence as a judgment or attribution about oneself or others; (b) intelligence in the form of working with others; (c) relationships between social settings and the development or display of intelligent behaviors. The final paragraphs note implications for testing.

Intelligence as a Judgment or Attribution

Rather than think of intelligence as a quality residing in the individual—possibly constant over time and universal in its definition—I would propose that we regard it as a judgment or attribution, comparable to the daily judgments we make about people being physically attractive, well-informed, witty, articulate, friendly, or shy. In all these other judgments, we are readily aware of the relativity of standards, of the likelihood of consensus about extreme cases, and the possibility of bias. Why should judgments about intelligence be any different?

Once we consider intelligence as an attribution, what research follows? Suppose we start from the stance of a person judging others (judgments about one's own ability involve some special biases). One would like to know first about the judge's categories. Is the range, for instance, restricted to "smart" and "dumb," or does it include such categories as "slick," "slow but thoughtful," "original," "too smart for his or her own good"? How do such differentiations come to be made?

Next one would wish to know about the bases of assignment to various categories (the cues, signs, or prototypes used) and, to add a developmental concern, about the ideas people in various social groups hold about the development of intelligence. Is ability in a given area thought to be something one can make early predictions about, or can it be assessed only relatively late in childhood? Is there a concept of "earlier is better," of "late bloomers," or—to quote a Chinese saying—of "early ripe, early rot"?

None of these questions is unanswerable. Some experimental possibilities have already been demonstrated (Goodnow, in press a, cites several definitional studies), and others may be readily borrowed from studies of attribution.

What of the other side of the picture, seen from the position of the person being judged? We need a great deal more information about the nature and acquisition of presentation rules for intelligent behaviors. What counts as a good display to one's peers or senior? What gives rise to situations where the wiser course is to act dumb? How do people learn to ward off a negative judgment by an advance defense ("This is off the top of my head . . ."), and when to display or to hide effort? These are again not unanswerable questions. Goodnow's (1976) dissection of "good" displays on intelligence tests is one route. Sternberg and Suben's (in press) analysis of professional socialization is another. Heath's (1983) insightful accounts of children's "ways with words" in three U.S. communities is a third.

Intelligence in Working with Others

Judgments about ability should cover situations where people interact with one another and/or solve problems together. As many scholars have pointed out, most testing situations are odd. One is asked questions to which the questioner already knows the answer. The questioner, however friendly, may not be asked for help. The solution should be generated—in the style of Rodin's Thinker—without access to physical or social props.

These features make it difficult to export many of our testing procedures to groups where other social rules operate. They also may give rise to faulty assessments of people within our own culture (e.g., McDermott, Cole, & Hood, 1978). More subtly, they have left us short of knowledge about the ways in which people display intelligence in run-of-the-mill situations. Not surprisingly, we now have a spurt of interest in intelligence that is "everyday" (Rogoff & Lave, 1984), "practical" (Sternberg & Wagner, in press), or "social" (Goodnow, in press b), and in situations where people work together (e.g., Fischer & Bullock, 1984; Griffin & Cole, 1984).

How can one turn such concerns into specific research topics? One route consists of observing how people operate when they are allowed to use other people's skills as resources (e.g., Cole & Traupmann, 1980; Griffin & Cole, 1984). Another is to observe interactions between more and less expert performers, especially when the more expert aim at transferring skill to the less expert (Rogoff & Wertsch, 1984, provide many examples), or when two or more people with varying skills and perspectives are required to reach a consensus (e.g., Doise, Mugny, & Perret-Clermont, 1975). A third is to ask about the processes and skills involved in the delegation of tasks or the negotiating of divisions of labor (Goodnow, in press b).

Social Setting and Intelligence

I begin with a problem underlined by Rogoff (1982) and by Valsiner (in press). Usually we proceed by thinking in terms of two separate variables (the individual with a set of predispositions or capacities, and an environment with some particular features) and then proceed to attempt the specification of how these two interact. Is there a way to start with concepts or procedures that from the start embody the interdependence of the two, or do not separate them? Rogoff (1982) describes such approaches as "contextual," offering as examples Gibson's concept of "affordances" and Vygotsky's concept of a "zone of proximal development."

To date, the number and range of such concepts is small. Their development seems critical. In the meantime, there are several problems to be worked on in the more separatist mode.

One is a more effective description of social environments and the opportunities they provide. Most descriptions of the world met by children present it as benignly disposed towards the acquisition of abilities, with limits to development placed mainly by the child's ability to comprehend what is available. The reality may be different (Goodnow, Knight, & Cashmore, in press).

A second is the need for the development of some common languages in the descriptions of social settings and of "intelligent" behaviors. Most of the time it is difficult to map one onto the other. Socioeconomic levels, for instance, do not map in any conceptual way onto performance levels on intelligence tests. It is more promising to ask how far the question-answer exchange in intelligence testing reflects what is practiced in other situations (e.g. Harkness & Super, 1977; Sternberg & Suben, in press), or to consider development as the acquisition of a view of options and pathways that approximates those in the outside world (Goodnow, in press c). More promising also is exploration of the extent to which environments provide various forms of social marking for logical relationships (e.g., familiar social situations that parallel and can "anchor" the learning of new connections between objects of propositions: cf. Doise, in press).

A third need is for more attention to coordinating the current variety of hypotheses about how social settings influence the development and display of intelligent behaviors. From various scholars come hypotheses about the role of social conflict, disequilibration, demands for adaptation, generalizations from initially specific learning, guided reinvention, supportive others, scaffolding, and direct instruction. We need to ask more closely about the evidence needed to choose among such hypotheses and about the criteria needed to determine how far one hypothesis is like another.

Implications for Intelligence Testing

I have left this issue to the last. I clearly feel that we have a great deal to do in the way of putting our theoretical house in order. If we are to test for something, we should surely have a clearer sense of what that something is.

A further reservation comes from the way in which test scores usually reflect and perpetuate the social order. They tend to consist of behaviors judged to be intelligent by a dominant social group whose members are likely to have had the greater practice in learning the behaviors and the display rules. If the function of testing is to predict who may most readily "pass" into that social group, the tests may be useful especially if they concentrate on items where tester and testee share some agreement about the validity of procedures. They may also be less excluding than the blanket judgment that no member of a nondominant group could possibly be bright. I would certainly, however, like to see a closer examination of assumptions about the social value of various forms of testing and of any attempt at prediction: assumptions, for example, about the importance of "maximizing potential" and avoiding "underdevelopment," and about the presence of limited places "at the top" (Goodnow, in press c). Why not a moratorium until we know more clearly what we are trying to predict, and what the costs and benefits are of various ways of proceeding?

REFERENCES

Doise, W. (in press). Social regulations in cognitive operations. In R.A. Hinde & A.N. Perret-Clermont (Eds.), *Relationships and cognitive development.* Oxford: Oxford University Press.

Doise, W., Mugny, G., & Perret-Clermont, A.N. (1975). Social interaction and the development of cognitive operations. *European Journal of Social Psychology, 5,* 367–383.

Fischer, K., & Bullock, D. (1984). Cognitive development in middle childhood. In W.A. Collins

(Ed.), *Development during middle childhood* (pp. 70–145). Washington, DC: National Education Association.

Goodnow, J.J. (1976). The nature of intelligent behaviour: Questions raised by cross-cultural studies. In L.B. Resnick (Ed.), *The nature of intelligence* (pp. 169–188). Hillsdale, NJ: Erlbaum.

Goodnow, J.J. (in press a). On being judged intelligent. *International Journal of Psychology.*

Goodnow, J.J. (in press b). Organizing and re-organizing: Some lifelong everyday forms of intelligent behavior. In R.J. Sternberg & R. Wagner (Eds.), *Practical intelligence: Origins of competence in everyday life.* New York: Cambridge University Press.

Goodnow, J.J. (in press c). Discussant's comments for R.J. Sternberg & J. Suben, The socialization of intelligence. In M. Perlmutter (Ed.), *Theories of intelligence: Minnesota Symposium on Child Development* (Vol. 19). Hillsdale, NJ: Erlbaum.

Goodnow, J.J., Knight, R., & Cashmore, J. (in press). Adult social cognition: Implications of parents' ideas for approaches to development. In M. Perlmutter (Ed.), *Social cognition: Minnesota Symposium on Child Development* (Vol. 18). Hillsdale, NJ: Erlbaum.

Griffin, P., & Cole, M. (1984). Current activity for the future: the Zo-ped. In B. Rogoff & J. Wertsch (Eds.), *Children's learning in the zone of proximal development* (pp. 45–64). San Francisco, CA: Jossey-Bass.

Harkness, S., & Super, C. (1977). Why African children are so hard to test. *Annals of the New York Academy of Sciences, 285,* 326–331.

Heath, S.B. (1983). *Ways with words.* New York: Cambridge University Press.

McDermott, R.P., Cole, M., & Hood, L. (1978). "Let's try to make it a good day"—Not so simple ways. *Discourse Processes, 3,* 155–168.

Rogoff, B. (1982). Integrating context and cognitive development. In M. Lamb & A. Brown (Eds.), *Advances in developmental psychology* (Vol. 2, pp. 127–169). Hillsdale, NJ: Erlbaum.

Rogoff, B., & Lave, J. (Eds.). (1984). *Everyday cognition: Its development in social context.* Cambridge, MA: Harvard University Press.

Rogoff, B., & Wertsch, J. (Eds.). (1984). *The zone of proximal development.* San Francisco, CA: Jossey-Bass.

Sternberg, R.J., & Suben, J. (in press). The socialization of intelligence. In M. Perlmutter (Ed.), *Theories of intelligence: Minnesota Symposium on Child Development* (Vol. 19). Hillsdale, NJ: Erlbaum.

Sternberg, R.J., & Wagner, R. (Eds.). (in press). *Practical intelligence: Origins of competence in the everyday world.* New York: Cambridge University Press.

Valsiner, J. (Ed.). (in press). *The role of the individual subject in scientific psychology.* New York: Plenum.

16.

Some Thoughts About Intelligence

John Horn

University of Southern California

"What do I conceive intelligence to be?" This is rather like asking me: "What do I conceive invisible green spiders to be?" For current knowledge suggests to me that intelligence is not a unitary entity of any kind. Attempts to describe it are bound to be futile.

In making such statements, I do not take issue with the idea that science is made from abstractions—ideas that we should not expect to "see" (even with the equivalent of a microscope). Good scientific concepts need not represent palpable "things." Also, I do not want to suggest that there is nothing to which scientists (and others) refer when they speak of intelligence. The phenomena represented by the word "intelligence" are very real and important.

No, these are not my concerns. Science is mainly ideas—systems of concepts bound together in theory. There could be a good scientific concept of intelligence, but there isn't—at least not yet. The word "intelligence" denotes a medley of important events. But that's the problem. A medley is a mixture of different things, not a composition. There is no functional unity to the medleys (for there are many) to which we refer when we use the word "intelligence." Our science of human abilities is beyond a stage where such mixture-measures well serve the purposes of research. Ideas about intelligence have been superseded. There are better ideas.

Preparation of the manuscript was supported in part by grants from the National Institute of Aging (AG04704) and the National Institute of Child Health and Human Development (HD17552).

Let me change the metaphor and put the basic point in a slightly different way. Over the last 80 or so years intelligence has been defined rather in the way that a pudding or stew is defined. A pudding can represent almost any mixture of different foods, and intelligence can represent almost any mixture of abilities. In verbal definitions as well as in operational definitions, intelligence is defined as a hodgepodge. Each definition is a different hodgepodge. Some of the same ingredients appear in the different hodgepodges, but each involves some different ingredients as well. And the ingredients are mixed in different proportions. These points are amply demonstrated by the collection of essays of which this essay is a part.

We know what we are talking about when we refer to mixture-measures of intelligence, but we know it only in a very loose sense. Just as we must be vague in speaking about the nutritional value of pudding (because we don't know what might be in such a mixture), so we must be vague when we try to make dependable (lawful) statements about intelligence. Current knowledge about human abilities allows us to be less vague; by discarding the idea of intelligence and describing the contents of this pudding, we can improve our descriptions of the phenomena of intelligence.

In 1921, under the press of the mass action theory of brain function, there was reason to suppose that a functional unity was at the core of different expressions of intellectual abilities. But today multiple-process concepts of brain function point to a different model—a multiple intelligences model—for human abilities. The bulk of evidence from the behavioral sciences suggests that there are several quite distinct functions represented in what has been called intelligence. Thus it is that to talk about, or look for, one intelligence is to talk about, or search for, an invisible green spider.

It is possible that a functional unity can be found to underlie a particular combination of the many abilities that are said to represent intelligence. The theory developed by Spearman (1927) is the best attempt thus far to specify the necessary and (ideally) sufficient elements of such a functional unity. If it were to be verified that such a subset of human capacities can be isolated, and it was shown that the elements of this subset work together as a unit in function and are brought about through a unitary process of genetic and environmental influences, then we could speak of a good scientific concept of intelligence. But the extant evidence (e.g.; Horn, 1982, 1985a, 1985b) does not support Spearman's theory—at least not in the forms in which the theory has been interpreted. To act as if evidence does support such a theory, or, worse, to suppose that hodgepodge measures and definitions represent such a unitary concept of intelligence, is to divert research from quests that should follow from what is known. What is known points to a view that human intellectual capacity is made from distinct "intelligences," having different genetic and environmental determiners, serving different functions in personality, based on different phylogenetic and ontogenetic histories, and relating in usefully different ways in predictions of occupational, educational, adaptational, and adjustment outcomes (i.e., if the operational definitions of such outcomes are sufficiently refined; see McNemar, 1964).

We know, for example, that there are at least several different neurotransmitter systems, and that these are associated with distinct behavioral patterns of an intellectual kind (e.g., Dunant & Israel, 1985; Noback & Demarest, 1975). There is good reason to suppose that these functions have independent genetic foundations. At an opposite extreme, we know that functions of gross features of the brain—as represented by laterality, front-to-back, and bottom-to-top distinctions—have a number of distinct associations with behavioral patterns and psychopathologies (Horn, 1985a, 1985b). There is good reason to suppose that these features, too, are based on different sets of genetic determiners, representing different phylogenic origins. When we move away from physiological variables and look at environmental determinants—learning, acculturation, familial influences, and so forth—again we find that most of the evidence points to different sets of influences operating in different ways to produce different cognitive structures in different people.

There is comfort (as well as cultural inertia) involved in our retention of hodgepodge ideas about intelligence; for when we seek to distance ourselves from these ideas we encounter difficulties not only in comprehending the complexity of the phenomena, but also in deciding on a level of abstraction on which to focus research. The problem is to continue to reference the complexity of human intellectual capacity without returning to misleading hodgepodges. Research could be focused on particular tasks of, say, information processing and imaging (as discussed by several authors in Sternberg's, 1985, book), but there must be concern that in focusing on detail this strategy loses the broad figure of human intellectual capacity (Humphreys, 1979). On the other hand, to use concepts as broad as those of Gf-Gc theory (e.g., Horn, 1985a; Horn & Cattell, 1982) is to run the risk of working with hodgepodges that have the same limitations I have criticized in concepts of intelligence (Guilford, 1981).

I don't have great insights into how best to deal with these issues of focus. As do most people, researchers included, I tend to rationalize that my approach is best, but in my saner moments I question this rationalization. After listening patiently to my doubts, however, I reason that in developmental psychology particularly—and most particularly when a life-span perspective is taken—the best strategy for now is to keep most descriptive research focused on broad abilities for which there is evidence of distinct patterns of relationships with other important variables, such as age, injury and education. From this base we can send out sorties, as it were, to find out how these abilities, and the development of these abilities, can be understood in terms of particular processes (Horn, 1982, 1985a, 1985b; Horn, Donaldson & Engstrom, 1981).

The broad abilities that represent this focus (in Gf-Gc theory) can be described as follows.

- Visual thinking, Gv, displayed in tasks in which one must fluently and accurately (not necessarily rapidly) perceive spatial configurations and form spatial images, interpret how objects change as they move through space, and form correct perspectives of objects in relation to each other.
- Auditory thinking, Ga, indicated by facility in "chunking" streams of sounds, keeping these chunks in awareness, and anticipating an auditory form that can develop out of such streams.
- Short-term acquisition-retrieval, SAR, operationally defined by a factor among many of the tasks of information-processing research, including different measures of primary and secondary memory, working memory, span memory, and "information processing," as such.
- Long-term retrieval-storage, TSR, indicated by fluency and breadth of retrieval of information stored long (e.g., months) before, and by secondary and tertiary recall and recognition over periods of 1 to 5 minutes.
- Correct decision speediness, CDS, a quickness in providing correct answers to a variety of problems of comprehension, reasoning, and problem solving.
- Attentive speediness, Gs, a quickness in identifying elements, or distinguishing between elements, of a stimulus pattern, particularly when measured under press to maintain focused attention.
- Structured knowledge of a culture, Gc, manifested in breadth and depth of understanding of the culture, comprehension of communication and analytic systems (e.g., mathematics), awareness of conventional interpretations, and judgment that can be based on such understanding—wisdom.
- Reasoning flexibility under novel conditions, Gf, most similar (I think) to Spearman's concept of eduction of relations and correlates, manifested in inductive, deductive, conjuctive, disjunctive, and other forms of reasoning, and in a variety of tasks designed to indicate capacity for abstraction, provided the tasks do not mainly measure knowledge of a culture (as per Gc or TSR).

These concepts, and particularly the operational definitions we can make for them at this stage of research, are hodgepodges relative to concepts we might define at a lower level of abstraction, but they have a number of distinct properties of function and development. We have some verified theories to support their distinctiveness. They are operationally independent and have reliably independent distributions in individual differences, both in childhood and adulthood (which is not to say, of course, that they have zero intercorrelations). They have different aging trends over the life span. They have different validities for predicting educational and occupational achievements (although I have yet to make this case convincingly). Such (sparse) evidence as we have suggests that they have different relationships to neurological variables, and stem from different genetic determiners. Thus, they are based on evidence of relevance for construct validation (Cronbach, 1986). They provide a useful base at one level of abstraction for exploring analytic explanations at other levels of abstraction.

This last feature of these concepts points research in directions that are worthwhile (which is not to argue for what is best or most needed). Process analyses of Gf decline illustrates one form of such research (as summarized in, for example, Horn, 1985a). This work suggests that a decline of Gf in adulthood can be described, in part, in terms of specific capacities for concentration, maintaining close attention, dividing attention, holding information in awareness, not being thrown off by irrelevant information, but also not losing awareness of what might seem to be irrelevant. Such processes do not account for all of the aging decline of Gf, but they describe some of it. Another form of analytic study is illustrated by efforts to show how physiological variables can be fitted to a model represented by the broad concepts I have described (e.g., Horn & Risberg, 1985). Some of this work suggests, for example, that Gf decline stems, in part, from an accumulation of (perhaps small) neurological damages brought about by decreases in blood supply to sections of the brain that are particularly vulnerable to blood supply vicissitudes. We need to identify different lifestyles associated with different patterns of improvements and declines of the broad abilities of Gf-Gc theory.

My suggestion is that the kind of work I have just outlined should be continued and increased. I think it has a good chance of netting genuine improvement in our understanding of human intellectual functioning.

REFERENCES

Broadbent, D.E. (1966). The well ordered mind. *American Educational Research Journal, 3,* 281–295.
Cronbach, L.J. (1986). Construct validation after thirty years. In R. Linn (Ed.), *Intelligence: Measurement, theory and public policy.* Urbana: University of Illinois Press.
Detterman, D.K. (1980). Does "g" exist? *Intelligence, 6,* 99–108.
Dunant, Y., & Israel, M. (1985). The release of acetycholine. *Scientific American, 252,* 58–66.
Guilford, J.P. (1980). Fluid and crystallized intelligences: Two fanciful concepts. *Psychological Bulletin, 81,* 498–501.
Horn, J.L. (1982). The aging of human abilities. In B.B. Wolman (Ed.), *Handbook of developmental psychology.* New York: Prentice Hall.

Horn, J.L. (1985a). Remodeling old models of intelligence. In B.B. Wolman (Ed.), *Handbook of intelligence.* New York: Wiley.

Horn, J.L. (1985b). Intellectual ability concepts. In R.L. Sternberg (Ed.), *Advances in the psychology of human intelligence* (Vol. 3). Hillsdale, NJ: Erlbaum.

Horn, J.L., & Cattell, R.B. (1982). Whimsey and misunderstandings of Gf-Gc theory. *Psychological Bullitin, 91,* 623–633.

Horn, J.L., & Donaldson, G., & Engstrom, R. (1981). Apprehension, memory and fluid intelligence decline in adulthood. *Research on Aging, 3,* 33–84.

Horn, J.L., & Risberg, J. (1985). Blood flow in the brain and adulthood aging of cognitive functions. In H. Wold (Ed.), *Theoretical empiricism: A general rationale for scientific model-building.* Washington, DC: Paragon House.

Humphreys, L.G. (1962). The organization of human abilities. *American Psychologist, 17,* 475–483.

Humphreys, L.G. (1979). The construct of general intelligence. *Intelligence, 3,* 105–120.

McNemar, Q. (1964). Lost: Our intelligence? Why? *American Psychologist, 19,* 871–882.

Noback, C.R., & Demarest, R.J. (1975). *The human nervous system.* New York: McGraw-Hill.

Spearman, C. (1927). *The abilities of man: Their nature and measurement.* New York: Macmillan.

Sternberg, R.J. (Ed.). (1985). *Human abilities: An information processing approach.* New York: Freeman.

Sternberg, S. (1975). Memory scanning: New findings and current controversies. *Quarterly Journal of Experimental Psychology, 27,* 1–32.

17.

Describing the Elephant

Lloyd G. Humphreys
University of Illinois

It is tempting to compare psychologists who discuss intelligence to the blind men, stationed at different parts of the animal's anatomy, who described an elephant. Not only do individual psychologists describe intelligence differently, but some act like blind men, not in touch with any part of the anatomy, who speculate on the ideal elephant or the intrinsic qualities of elephantness. What these qualities should be may be a problem for some people, but not for scientists. A beginning toward the description of the whole elephant is a scientific goal that can be achieved by the interested parties if they are willing to accept a minimal constraint and to collaborate with each other. Of course, the description will be limited by the research information available, but this is characteristic of the scientific enterprise.

The necessary constraint is to recognize that we are all *observing* the elephant. Even though our individual observations are limited, I believe that it will turn out that we are all observing the same elephant. Some features of the elephant are more difficult to observe than others, but we are not restricted to unaided sensory input. We can be aided by instruments, but unobservables cannot be included.

The distinction between phenotype and genotype is useful, even when one has little dependable information about genotype. The task is to describe the elephant phenotypically. Observable traits can contain independent, correlated, and interactive genetic and environmental contributions to variance, but the description itself is independent of its causes. The phenotypic description of an elephant is more complex than is indicated by the elephant's size alone. One must include the behavioral, biochemical, and physiological processes as well as the anatomical structures in the description. Some may wish to include the elephant's environmental niche as well.

The elephant of intelligence may be so complex that we can and should decide to add a modifier to the term *intelligence* for each of the several ways in which the elephant can be described. No one aspect is sufficient to encompass the elephant of intelligence. If we could agree on appropriate modifiers, it would be easier to communicate with each other, with scientists in other disciplines, and with the general public. I shall now sketch some of these possibilities.

Although I may be biased by my own publications (Humphreys, 1971, 1979, 1981), I believe that a consensus on one such intelligence can be reached by starting with the characteristics of behavioral measurement in general and with the behaviors sampled by tests of intelligence such as the Stanford–Binet and the several Wechsler scales. Intelligence, or at least one part of the elephant, is defined as the repertoire of intellectual knowledge and skills available to the person at a particular point in time. Intellectual is defined by the consensus among experts, as revealed by the continuity in types of items that appear in standard tests of intelligence dating from 1905 to the present. A consensus concerning the limits of the intellectual domain can and should change as research findings accumulate, but a priori speculation is not a sufficient basis for change.

Phenotypic intelligence should be measured as physical traits are measured: in a metric that allows for growth or decay over time. A converted score defined as height relative to chronological age is a useful addition to the linear scale for height, but relative height is not primary. Phenotypic height increases with age, but whether a given relative score such as a height quotient changes with age is a separate research question. Neither does converting a measure of height to a quotient produce a measure of capacity for growth.

A ratio scale for intelligence is not on the horizon, but an approximation to an interval scale is within the present state of the art. A scale that describes growth is needed for clarity in conceptualizing intelligence as a phenotypic trait. It is also needed by many persons doing research with subjects having a range of chronological age who are growing or decaying at nontrivial rates. Identifying intelligence with a relative measure has been confusing and has led to numerous errors in research design and analysis.

The view of intelligence just described can be thought of as a *content* description. It relates the nature of the items in the test to the content of the person's repertoire. The latter, however, is acquired, and the acquisition and utilization can be described in terms of *processes*. These can also be defined phenotypically. How are intellectual skills and knowledge acquired, stored, retrieved, and generalized? Either view of the elephant is incomplete without the other.

A good deal less is known about intelligence as process than as content, but research output is growing at a rapid rate. There are too many contributors to attempt a listing. From the perspective of individual differences in processes, recommendations can be made about how this research should be conducted. The most important of these is to study relationships among various ways of measuring a given process, among different processes, and between processes and content measures of intelligence.

Research on individual differences requires more power than that necessary to reject a population correlation of zero. Degree of correlation needs to be determined within fairly narrow confidence intervals. This means inevitably that samples have to be large. Use of extreme groups on one of the two variables correlated does increase power to test the hypothesis of a zero population correlation, but this design makes it difficult to do more than determine the sign of the correlation. A design that is useful for exploratory research should be abandoned and the entire range of individual differences substituted. Sampling from the population of undergraduate college students should also be supplemented by sampling from a wider range of human talent.

A more subtle problem can be described as an example of the Campbell–Fiske multitrait-multimethod methodology. How much variance in the distribution of responses is contributed by the choice of dependent variable or by the choice of method of measurement? I believe that, with high generality, there is a great deal of unique variance in responses to a particular stimulus in a particular setting. In order to infer that a given process is involved, the process should be measured with a variety of content in a variety of ways. It is useful to conceptualize variance in terms of common and unique factors even if one never uses the factor-analytic methodology. We need to recognize that psychology is necessarily a multivariate discipline and to plan our research accordingly.

The study of communality among different processes and between process and repertoire requires that the measures from which process is inferred be psychometrically sound. Each measure must meet standards of internal consistency and reliability before small correlations can be interpreted as little communality or its obverse, high specificity. Reverting to an earlier discussion, the sample must also be sufficiently large and from a population having a sufficient range of talent that an obtained correlation near zero will have a sufficiently small confidence interval before specificity can be concluded. The same is true for large correlations and a conclusion that generality has been found.

A third approach to the description of the elephant is the ecological one. The task is to describe phenotypically effective behaviors in a given sociocultural setting. This approach includes both content and process as well as traits that are ordinarily labelled motivation and personality (Gardner, 1983; Sternberg, 1984). As a matter of fact, size, strength, sensory acuity, muscular coordination, and possibly others might be included. Pushed just a little, this concept comes close to Darwinian reproductive fitness. The inclusion of too much under the rubric of intelligence may be counterproductive for research and theory. My priority is to find out more about the interrelationships between intelligence as content and as process. If those phenotypic constructs are properly interpreted, one does not need the umbrella construct to be able to equate for social purposes the intelligence levels of different ethnic groups. The message that there is nothing fundamentally wrong in the ecological intelligence of an ethnic group may actually detract from the need to correct for important phenotypic differences in content or process required in a broader socio-cultural context.

REFERENCES

Gardner, H. (1983). *Frames of mind.* New York: Basic Books.
Humphreys, L.G. (1971). Theory of intelligence. In R. Cancro (Ed.), *Intelligence: Genetic and environment influences* (pp. 31–42). New York: Grune & Stratton.
Humphreys, L.G. (1979). The construct of general intelligence. *Intelligence, 3,* 105–120.
Humphreys, L.G. (1981). The primary mental ability. In M.P. Friedman, J.P. Das, and N. O'Connor (Eds.), *Intelligence and learning* (pp. 87–102). New York: Plenum.
Sternberg, R.J. (1984). Toward a triarchic theory of human intelligence. *The Behavioral and Brain Sciences, 7,* 269–315.

18.

The Heffalump of Intelligence

Earl Hunt

The University of Washington

In one of the episodes of A. A. Milne's philosophic novel, Pooh and Piglet track a heffalump. In fact, though, they are tracking themselves in the snow. Now Pooh can be forgiven, for he was a Bear of Very Little Brain. But what about psychologists?

The participants in a NATO-sponsored Advanced Study Institute in December of 1984 debated the general versus the specific nature of intelligence, the rules of biological and cultural determinism, and the extent to which intelligence should be defined by individual characteristics in social context.

The same topics were raised in a 1921 symposium. Did psychologists fail to explore them? Hardly. The writers in 1921 proposed numerous research projects intended to answer the questions. By and large, these projects were finished. Why do the questions remain? Should the nonscientist draw an unpleasant conclusion about brain size in psychologists?[1]

Is the situation really this bad? There are different opinions about progress in understanding intelligence. Eysenck (1973) viewed intelligence testing as a major scientific breakthrough. Kamin (1974) described the

This research was supported by ONR contract #N00014-84-K-5553 to the University of Washington, Earl Hunt, Principal Investigator. He is happy to acknowledge this support. The opinions expressed are the author's and do not express those of the Office of Naval Research or the Department of the Navy.

[1]Psychologists may have an excuse. In the 1921 symposium Louis Terman stated that research programs should be funded at $100,000 a year, and indirect costs had not even been invented. In 1984 dollars (with indirect costs) that is about $850,000. Were we underfunded or are we scientists of Very Little Brain?

same work with statements that border on charges of fraud. The argument revolves around two broad issues: What causes intelligence, and what does intelligence do? This paper outlines an approach that may guide research on the first question, and emphatically denies that the second has any meaning.

The Definition of Intelligence

The approach is based on two dogma. The first is that intelligence should be studied within the framework of a theory of cognition. Cognition, in turn, will be defined as a computation on an internal mental representation. Extensive treatments of this view and its ramifications are available (Johnson-Laird, 1983; Pylyshyn, 1983), so no detailed argument for it will be presented here. A computational approach to thinking stresses the role of theory, since internal representations are, by definition, unobservable events. Therefore, any discussion of individual differences in thinking must take place in the context of assumptions about the nature of mental representations and the computations that can be executed on them.

Of course, one's theory could be wrong. But what is the alternative? Discussions of intelligence always take place in the context of an explicit or an implicit theory of cognition, and implicit theories are as likely to be wrong as are explicit theories. It is just harder to see that they are wrong.

The second dogma is that intelligence must be defined in the context of a particular set of mental actions that are believed to follow common laws. The decision to treat particular actions as a collective could be made on the basis of cognitive theory, as in the case of different paradigms for studying memory, or it could be made because of the practical importance of the collective, as in the case of the set of actions that must be performed by an air traffic controller. The importance of choosing the right set of actions will be discussed below, but for the moment suppose that they have been defined. Performance will be a function of two classes of variables: variations in the conditions under which thinking take place (lighting, time pressure, time of day, etc.), and variations in the characteristics of the individual thinkers (age, sex, and ultimately, individual identity).

"Intelligence" is solely a shorthand term for the variation in competence on cognitive tasks that is statistically associated with personal variables, either as main effects or as interaction terms. This is an extremely pragmatic, unreified definition. Intelligence is used as a collective term for "demonstrated individual differences in mental competence." Furthermore, since variation is a population concept, an individual cannot have "intelligence," although an individual can possess specific competencies. This definition is at odds with the colloquial definition of "intelligence" (Sternberg et al., 1981), but so what? The colloquial definition does not seem to have led to great scientific clarity.

Context-sensitive definitions of intelligence can be generalized, provided that the basis of the generalization is clear. Formal statistical generalization is warranted only if both the tasks and the participants represent a random sample from some well-defined universe of human society. While such research is logically possible, it is virtually never done. Instead, more informal procedures are used. The most common is to make an intuitive job analysis of cognitive behavior in the sector of the "real world" that is the target of generalization, and to create a job sample on the basis of the intuitive analysis. (This is what Binet and Simon did.) Generalization is by rhetoric, which is not terrible, provided that it is made clear that one's confidence in the generality of the findings is based on subjective probability.

A more respectable way of generalizing the results of empirical studies is to select the tasks, and in some cases, the people studied, on the basis of a theory of cognitive action. Results can be generalized based on a taxonomy of theoretically similar and dissimilar tasks. But what would generate the task taxonomy? Again, reasonable progress depends upon having a theory of cognition.

Before presenting such a theory, one more implication of the general approach will be mentioned. If intelligence is to be used to refer to population variation in performance, then intelligence can never be used as a causal variable. It makes no sense to say that Jones became a professor while Smith became a sales manager because Jones was more intelligent than Smith, or vice versa. It may make sense to say that Jones possessed a penchant for abstract thinking and risk aversion, while Smith was a rapid decision maker with a good ability to judge the reactions of others in social situations. These are specific skills which can have antecedents and consequences. Collectively, the antecedents are causes of intelligence. Intelligence, being a population concept, cannot cause individual behaviors.

Intelligence in a Computational Theory

Since people are biological devices, it is a truism that individual differences in physiological mechanisms must, ultimately, be the basis of all individual differences in mental competency. Whether or not a particular competency is usefully thought of at the biological level is quite another matter. It is equally a truism that a great deal of human behavior is determined at the level of specific, consciously executed strategies. A great deal of human problem solving takes place at that level. Here is where we see overt educational and cultural differences, including the particular subcultural differences that have recently been associated with subject matter expertise.

A computational theory captures this distinction because computational theories are theories of the manipulation of *physical* symbol systems (Newell, 1980). A computational theory highlights a third level of information processing intervening between the biological and the conscious strategic level. Pylyshyn (1983) has referred to it as the "functional architecture" level, by analogy to the functional architecture of actual computing systems. I prefer a somewhat more familiar computer-based analogy. In actuality, computer programs are written in a language that contains certain primitive operators, such as the familiar arithmetical operations of the FORTRAN and BASIC languages. The power of the primitive operations will partly determine the performance of a computer program. In more psychological terms, the conscious strategies that we follow must depend upon the execution of primitive information-processing operations. The ways in which these operations are executed are transparent to us, just as the manner of execution of computing primitives is transparent to the programmer.

Intelligence depends on performance at all three levels. Between-level interactions occur and are important. The biological level establishes the limits of efficiency of the elementary processes. The elementary processes in turn set limits on the complexity of the conscious strategies that can be executed. To illustrate, an excellent case can be made for the proposal that choosing between alternative responses is a basic step in cognition—that this is an elementary step that limits the speed of cognitive processing. The evidence for this rests on the fact that there are moderate but reliable correlations between choice-reaction latencies and performance on such varied and complex tasks as the Raven Matrix test (Jensen & Munro, 1979) and tests of reading comprehension (Palmer et al., 1985). There is also a sizable body of evidence linking elevated choice-reaction times to cardiovascular malfunction and to decreased oxygenation of the brain (Spirduso, 1980). Such observations support a "bottom-up" model of cognition, in which biology limits information processing, which in turn limits the conscious strategies one can use. This is an extremely important point. Elementary information-processing functions connect the brain to the mind. Some connections may be very general ones, such as "efficiency of information transmission in the central nervous system," which would be analogous to circuit reliability, while others may be specialized, such as "mental rotation of visual images," which is more analogous to a specific arithmetical operation that is used in only some programs. Tracing out the detailed use of both specific and general information-processing actions is a topic for empirical research. Such research will lead to a picture of intelligence.

The picture is certainly complex. Lower levels of cognition provide

ranges of strategies that can be executed at higher levels. Within these
ranges, the choice of a permitted strategy can have a great deal of influence
on cognitive competence. What is even more interesting, and what makes a
theory of intelligence inevitably more complex, is that conscious strategies
can alter the demands that a task makes upon elementary information-
processing capacities and, through them, upon biological capacity. Examples abound. Mnemonists free themselves from limits on short-term memory capacity (Chase & Ericsson, 1981). People from different cultures may
approach the same task as an exercise in verbal or visual memory (Kearins,
1981). The flexibility of the human cognitive system is a sufficient reason to
refuse to say "What causes intelligence?" A far better question is "How are
individual differences displayed in this or that class of cognitive tasks?" Such
questions cannot be answered by assigning a person a number based upon
that person's relative standing in a population. The conventional IQ score
has no place in a computational theory of intelligence.

Implications for Major Issues

In a computational theory, a person's "intelligence" is simply the collection
of cognitive skills the person possesses. Jensen (1984) and Eysenck (1973)
and other proponents of the view of a general trait theory of intelligence
usually cite the statistical evidence for a g factor as the major evidence
against a "collection of skills" position. This is an intuitively compelling
argument. But is it valid? The evidence for g rests on the statistical observation of a *positive manifold*—tests of intellectual functioning are almost
always positively correlated with each other. Snow, Kyllonen, and Marshalek
(1984) have used multidimensional scaling techniques to produce a conceptual space of intelligence tests, based on the correlations between them.
The more complex, "g-loaded" tests lie in the center of the space. Tests of
specialized information-processing functions lie in the periphery. The overall configuration is rather like a wheel, with spokes representing specific
classes of ability (verbal, spatial, etc.) radiating out from the center. This
configuration would be expected if performance on complex tests were
based on the aggregation of performance on more and more elementary
tasks. The more complex two tests, the more they would be likely to depend on common elementary components, and hence the higher the correlation between them. On the other hand, there would be no one elementary component controlling any complex task, and hence correlations
between individual components and complex tests should be reliable but
not large. Put another way, positive manifold is not "just" a statistical artifact; it is a phenomenon that has a psychological cause. But positive manifold does not compel one to believe in g.

The same argument can be made with respect to elementary tasks and biological measures. Many functions that are considered elementary at the information-processing level are certainly complex at the biological level. For instance, the well known memory scanning paradigm devised by S. Sternberg (1966) involves both the visual and the linguistic information-processing system. Correlations between tests of different elementary information-processing functions should depend upon the number of common physical systems that underlie them. One could conduct a multidimensional analysis of elementary tasks that was similar to the analysis of intelligence tests by Snow et al. Would the resulting configuration have a physiological explanation? We do not know.

The computational approach to cognition encourages the development of models of performance on specific cognitive tasks. A theoretical rationale is crucial. There is little scientific point in collecting correlations between two poorly understood tasks, even if one of them has been labeled an intelligence test. Far more may be learned by studying the correlations between two tasks that are understood, in order to isolate individual differences in specific aspects of cognitive functioning. This is not an attack on the collection of correlations for use in predicting personal performance in industrial and educational settings. Such studies seek correlations in order to use them, so a measure can be justified solely on the basis of its statistical properties. The scientific analysis of individual differences in mental competencies should be driven by specific models of how those competencies are produced, and the measures taken should be justified in terms of those theories.

Given this view, the computational approach to intelligence is somewhat counter to the drive to "apply science to the real world." Perhaps the study of intelligence has suffered from too much of an emphasis on application. Rather than single out a particular content area for more research, I prefer to close with a plea for better, more disciplined theoretical analyses. Rather than try to produce ever vaster, ever vaguer philosophic approaches, let us go about the tedious, necessary job of building precise models, verifying them, and thus uniting theories of intelligence with theories of cognition.

REFERENCES

Chase, G., & Ericsson, K.A. (1981). Skilled memory in cognitive skills and their acquisition. In J. Anderson (Ed.), *Cognitive skills and their acquisition* (pp. 141–189). Hillsdale, NJ: Erlbaum.

Eysenck, H.J. (1973). *The inequality of man.* London: Temple Smith.

Jensen, A.R. (1984). Test validity: g versus the specificity doctrine. *Journal of Social and Biological Structures, 7,* 93–118.

Jensen, A.R., & Munro, E. (1979). Reaction time, movement time, and intelligence. *Intelligence, 3,* 121–126.

Johnson-Laird, P.N. (1983). *Mental models.* Cambridge, MA: Harvard University Press.

Kamin, L. (1974). *The science and politics of I.Q.* Hillsdale, NJ: Erlbaum.

Kearins, J.M. (1981). Visual spatial memory in Australian aboriginal children. *Cognitive Psychology, 13,* 434–460.

Newell, A. (1980). Physical symbol systems. *Cognitive Science, 4*(2), 135–183.

Palmer, J., MacLeod, C., Hunt, E., and Davidson, J. (1984). Information processing correlates of reading. *Journal of Verbal Learning and Verbal Behavior, 24,* 59–88.

Pylyshyn, Z.W. (1984). *Computation and cognition.* Cambridge, MA: Bradford Books, MIT Press.

Snow, R.E., Kyllonen, P.C., and Marshalek, B. (1984). The topography of ability and learning correlations. In R.J. Sternberg (Ed.), *Advances in the psychology of human intelligence* (Vol. 2, pp. 47–88). Hillsdale, NJ: Erlbaum.

Spirduso, W.W. (1980). Physical fitness, aging, and psychomotor speed: A review. *Journal of Gerontology, 14*(6), 850–865.

Sternberg, R.J., Conway, B.E., Ketron, J.L., & Bernstein, M. (1981). People's conceptions of intelligence. *Journal of Personality and Social Psychology, 41,* 37–55.

Sternberg, S. (1966). High speed scanning in human memory. *Science, 153,* 652–654.

19.

Intelligence: "Definition," Measurement, and Future Research

Arthur R. Jensen
University of California, Berkeley

First, some definitions: A *mental test* consists of a number of *items.* An *item* is a *cognitive task* on which a person's performance can be *objectively* scored, that is, classified ("right" or "wrong" = 1 or 0), or graded on a scale (e.g., "poor," "fair," "good," "excellent" = 0, 1, 2, 3), or counted (e.g., number of digits recalled, number of parts of a puzzle fitted together within a given time limit), or measured on a ratio scale (e.g., reaction time or the time interval between presentation and completion of a task). In order to measure individual differences in a given group of people, item difficulty (i.e., percent "failing" the item) must be greater than 0 and less than 100%. By *objective* is meant that there is a high level of agreement among different observers in their scoring of an individual's performance on a given task. (As in all types of precise measurement, a high level of agreement, or objectivity, may depend upon special training of the observers.) By *mental* and *cognitive* is simply meant that (a) very little, if any, of the individual differences variance in performance is associated with individual differences in sheer physical capacity, such as sensory acuity or muscular strength; (b) very little, if any, of the variance in item difficulty is associated with physical capacities: In other words, there is negligible interaction (or correlation) between individual differences in physical capacities and differences in item difficulty. The *requirements* of the task must be understood by the testee through proper instructions by the tester. This can be objectively assessed by the testee's demonstrating adequate performance on simple exemplaries of the same type of task. The individual's score on a test is the sum of the scores on each of the items that compose the test.

Such tests can be made up in great variety, involving different sensory and response modalities; different media (words, numbers, symbols, pictures of familiar things, objects); different types of task requirements (discrimination, generalization, recall, naming, verbal expression, manipulation of objects, comparison, decision, inference, etc.); and varying complexity, ranging all the way from one- or two-choice reaction-time tasks up to inductive and deductive reasoning problems. The variety of items and item types is limited only by the ingenuity of the inventors of test items.

A collection of such items in a test, when administered to an unrestricted or representative sample of the general population of children or adults, shows generally low positive correlations among virtually all the items on which there is some reliable variance. Individual differences variance in test scores is contributed mostly by the item covariances; the proportion of the total test variance contributed by the item covariances is known as the test's *internal consistency reliability,* or *homogeneity.*

When any large (10 or more) collection of tests of diverse item types is administered to a representative sample of the population, the tests show substantially higher positive intercorrelations than do the items. Provided that all items were scored such that better performance receives the higher score, there are virtually no negative or zero correlations found among mental tests in an unrestricted sample. This empirical fact indicates a common source of variance in all cognitive tests.

Factor analysis affords quantitative estimates of the relative degree to which variance on each of the various tests in a particular collection of tests is "loaded" with the source of variance that is common to all of the tests in the collection. This common source of variance can be termed a *general factor,* or simply *g.* The first principal component, the first principal factor, and the highest order factor in a hierarchical analysis can all represent the *g* factor more or less equally well.

The *g* factor in a large collection of diverse mental tests is a scientifically and practically useful "working definition" of *intelligence.* The *g* will differ somewhat from one collection of tests to another, of course, but by selecting diverse tests with the highest *g* loadings in each collection, one can obtain a battery of tests whose *g* is maximally correlated with the *g* of many other collections of diverse tests. The most highly *g*-loaded tests may well be much less diverse in type than tests in general, and only a relatively few highly *g*-loaded tests can measure *g* as reliably as a relatively large collection of tests picked at random from all existing or possible tests. For most practical purposes, even a single reliable test with a high *g* loading may serve as a satisfactory measure of *g.* The most highly *g*-loaded tests usually involve some form of relation eduction or relatively complex mental transformations or manipulations of the stimulus input in order to achieve the correct response. The best "intelligence" tests for practical purposes are those that are both the most highly g-loaded and the most appropriate for the particular population and circumstances in which they are to be used. Many "IQ" tests also measure other factors besides g, for example, such "group factors" as verbal, spatial, numerical, memory, and so forth. There is no harm in this, for practical purposes, because these group factors seldom detract from the predictive validity of the test. For certain research purposes, it may be necessary to get rid of the non-g variance, which can be achieved by using a battery of diverse tests and extracting g factor scores, or regressing out other factors. Whether or not one wishes to include *every* kind of cognitive ability in addition to g under the label *intelligence* is of no real consequence, although for scientific purposes it seems preferable to retain legitimate distinctions, and if the term *intelligence* is used at all, I think it best to identify it with g rather than with some unknown amalgam of other abilities in addition to g.

Why the focus on g, or the first principal factor, rather than on some other factor(s), rotated or not? First is the fact that g is the single largest source of individual differences in all cognitive activities that involve some degree of mental complexity and that eventuate in behavior which can be measured in terms of some objective standard of performance. Also, g carries far more predictive weight than any other single factor or combination of other factors (independent of g) in its practical validity for predicting the performance of individuals in school and college, in armed forces training programs, and in employment in business and industry.

The fact that the g factor is more highly related than any other factor to variables whose origin and measurement are entirely independent of factor analysis, such as choice reaction time, the average evoked potential, and inbreeding depression, means that g is a construct with theoretical significance which extends beyond the mathematical operations involved in its extraction from the intercorrelations among psychometric variables. There are also many physical correlates of g (e.g., stature, brain size, myopia, blood type, body chemistry), but their meaning is still obscure.

Research on g can proceed in two directions; both are scientifically valuable. Going in one direction, we can discover and study all the various "real-life" manifestations and correlates of g and their educational, occupational, economic, and social significance. And we can study how the g resources of a society affect its general welfare and the quality of life of its members. It is already known that g is implicated in many socially significant phenomena; these warrant further systematic investigation. Although it is scientifically unimportant whether or not g resembles the layman's notions of "intelligence" (which are open-ended and unclearly specified), it is of scientific interest to study popular conceptions of intelligence and their relationship to g.

Going in the other, reductionist direction, we can investigate the correlations of *g* with the concepts and measurements derived from the experimental and chronometric analysis of elementary cognitive processes. Research has already shown that individual differences in information *processes* (as contrasted with the *content* of the information) constitute a large proportion of the variance in the *g* of standard psychometric tests. The established high heritability of individual differences in *g* indicates that there is a biological substrate of *g,* presumably in the neural structure and physiology of the cerebral cortex. It has been found that the magnitude of the correlations between certain features of the brain's evoked electrical potentials and various psychometric tests is directly related to the tests' *g* loadings.

One of the main tasks of future research on *g* is to pursue a reductionist type of investigation still further toward the goal of achieving a scientifically satisfactory exploration of *g* in terms of its physical substrate and of how environmental influences affect its development. Other main topics calling for further systematic research concern the ontogeny of *g* in terms of the development of information processes and their biological substrates, the evolution of *g* in the human species, and the genetic architecture of *g.* The same kind of investigative treatment should also be accorded to the major group factors that constitute other important aspects of mental ability There are enough scientifically open questions in this domain to keep many research psychologists fully occupied well into the next century.

20.

Intelligence: The Interaction of Culture and Cognitive Processes

James W. Pellegrino

University of California, Santa Barbara

The term *intelligence* denotes the general concept that individuals' responses to situations vary in quality and value as judged by their culture. Such overt behaviors result from covert mental processes and events. This leads to vague, general definitions of intelligence referring to mental processes or capacities. Examples include the ability to learn, to reason and solve problems, or to adapt to one's environment. Definitions such as these always need expansion and qualification. First, not all types of learning, reasoning, and adaptation are deemed equally important. Second, learning, reasoning, and adaptation are themselves general concepts requiring further specification. Given these and other definitional problems, we have opted for operational definitions involving performance differences among individuals on cognitive problems with cultural relevance and predictive utility. Cultural context shapes our implicit theories which then influence our explicit theories and judgments (see, e.g., Sternberg, Conway, Ketron, & Bernstein, 1981).

To understand the nature of intelligence we need to understand the nature of human cognition as well as the nature of value systems within cultures. Intelligence is implicitly determined by the interaction of organisms' cognitive machinery and their sociocultural environment. Cross-cultural studies of human cognition have alerted us to the need to consider cultural values and context in any understanding of intelligence (e.g., Berry, 1981; Charlesworth, 1976; Keating, 1984). In Western society, we value behaviors closely associated with formal schooling. Thus, "academic intelligence" is prototypical of our concept (Neisser, 1976, 1979; Sternberg et al., 1981).

Current understanding of the nature of human cognition is a product of three relatively distinct approaches to studying the phenomenon. One approach has focused on the mental structures and processes underlying individual performance on specific types of problems. A second approach has focused on patterns of individual change in problem solution over the course of cognitive development. The third approach has focused on patterns of individual differences in the accuracy of solving diverse sets of problems. The outcomes and implications of information-processing, developmental, and differential approaches have remained largely unintegrated (Kail & Pellegrino, 1985). However, conclusions about the nature of human cognition can be derived from these three approaches. First, mental events can be described and studied in terms of an organized system of structures, processes, and specific knowledge. These three elements differentially combine and interact to determine performance in any given situation. Second, over the course of development, systematic changes occur in the organization, operation, and utilization of the basic elements of the cognitive system. Third, systematic variation exists between and within individuals in the elements, organization, and operation of the cognitive system.

Our understanding of the specifics of human cognition has increased considerably in recent years as a result of advances in theory and research on human information processing. Many basic processes for representing, transforming, combining, and comparing information have been specified. Progress has also been made in conceptualizing how information is represented and in specifying the types of information that individuals have at their disposal. Theories of cognition now capture some of the complexity of actual human cognition. This includes important insights into some of its limitations. It has also become clear that no single element of the system lies at the core of human cognition. There is, however, an aspect of cognition that seems particularly important. It has been variously labeled control processes, executive functions, and metacomponents (Sternberg, 1984a). All these labels refer to processes involved in the selection, organization, and monitoring of other individual processes. In current models of cognition, these executive functions are embedded in production system "programs."

To make further progress in understanding human cognition, we need an integration and elaboration of theory and research on human information processing. Only recently have such integrations been attempted (e.g., Anderson, 1983). Many issues are in need of resolution, such as the processes involved in creating mental representations of information, the types of representations that can be and are created, and the processes that then operate on such representations. Of equal or greater concern are the mechanisms by which basic operations are selected, organized, and sequenced in order to perform some task. The problem still remains of specifying the learning programs which assemble the performance programs (Simon, 1976) and some progress has been made (e.g., Anderson, 1982). Perhaps the most significant issue for theory and research is differentiating specific knowledge and processes for performing familiar tasks from general knowledge and processes for acquiring such knowledge and learning to perform novel tasks. Research addressing these aspects of human cognition must achieve a balance between nomothetic and ideographic approaches. Furthermore, research on these topics must consider how the same individual processes information in a variety of situations.

There are no simple answers to the question of what performances should be studied. They are partially determined by theory and by cultural values and context. Nevertheless, research on the nature of human cognition has progressed considerably in recent years by focusing on complex tasks with "ecological" validity. Examples include research on discourse processes, problem solving and reasoning in science and mathematics, the acquisition of knowledge in substantive domains, and solution of problems on conventional cognitive tests (see e.g., Sternberg, 1982, 1984b). Two benefits accrue from pursuing research in such domains. First, these domains force us to deal with the complexity, richness, and diversity of what humans know and can do. Second, the outcomes are of potential value for designing assessments of human cognitive skills and programs to modify and improve them.

Current mental tests provide global indications of a person's performance relative to others, rather than a rich description of a person's current cognitive capabilities. This reflects a historical orientation in assessment toward classification, prediction, and selection. While there is some utility in such an approach, the information obtained is weakly descriptive, with little diagnostic and prescriptive value. Ostensibly, we should want to test individuals to obtain information about their specific cognitive skills. Such information can then be used to design environments that selectively adapt to and/or improve an individual's current skills. The goal of testing should be to provide diagnostic information that permits the design of programs to improve cognition (Glaser, 1981). If we accept this goal of testing, then extensive research must be conducted on reliable assessment of the components of cognition. Related research needs to be done on how and how much we can improve cognition.

Current mental tests indirectly assess many basic elements of cognition. These include semantic and quantitative knowledge, reasoning and problem solving with familiar and novel content, and the manipulation of visual-spatial information. I see no reason to discontinue assessing these elements of cognition, only the need to reorient methods of assessment to obtain reliable information about the processes and knowledge underlying performance. There is, however, a need to expand the range of knowledge and skills assessed. Many basic aspects of cognition are not tested simply because it is difficult to do so in traditional testing formats (see Hunt & Pellegrino, 1985). Aspects of cognition that need to be a part of future assessment procedures include the allocation of attention, executive functions, and learning processes. Current tests provide no information or very indirect assessments of these and other aspects of cognition. Thus, a major challenge is precise specification of the many different elements of cognition, including executive functions and learning processes, and the development of methods for their assessment.

REFERENCES

Anderson, J.R. (1982). Acquisition of cognitive skill. *Psychological Review, 89,* 369–406.

Anderson, J.R. (1983). *The architecture of cognition.* Cambridge, MA: Harvard University Press.

Berry, J.W. (1981). Cultural systems and cognitive styles. In M. Friedman, J.P. Das & N. O'Connor (Eds.), *Intelligence and learning* (pp. 395–405). New York: Plenum.

Charlesworth, W.R. (1976). Human intelligence as adaptation: An ethological approach. In L.B. Resnick (Ed.), *The nature of intelligence* (pp. 147–168). Hillsdale, NJ: Erlbaum.

Glaser, R. (1981). The future of testing. *American Psychologist, 36,* 923–936.

Hunt, E., & Pellegrino, J.W. (1985). Using interactive computing to expand intelligence testing: A critique and prospectus. *Intelligence, 9,* 207–236.

Kail, R., & Pellegrino, J.W. (1985). *Human intelligence: Perspectives and prospects.* New York: W.H. Freeman.

Keating, D.P. (1984). The emperor's new clothes: The "new look" in intelligence research. In R.J. Sternberg (Ed.), *Advances in the psychology of human intelligence* (Vol. 2, pp. 1–45). Hillsdale, NJ: Erlbaum.

Neisser, U. (1976). General, academic and artificial intelligence. In L.B. Resnick (Ed.), *The nature of intelligence* (pp. 135–144). Hillsdale, NJ: Erlbaum.

Neisser, U. (1979). The concept of intelligence. In R.J. Sternberg & D.K. Detterman (Eds.), *Human intelligence: Perspectives on its theory and measurement* (pp. 179–189). Norwood, NJ: Ablex.

Simon, H.A. (1976). Identifying basic abilities underlying intelligent performance of complex tasks. In L.B. Resnick (Ed.), *The nature of intelligence* (pp. 65–98). Hillsdale, NJ: Erlbaum.

Sternberg, R.J. (Ed.). (1982). *Advances in the psychology of human intelligence* (Vol. 1). Hillsdale, NJ: Erlbaum.

Sternberg, R.J. (1984a). Toward a triarchic theory of human intelligence. *Behavioral and Brain Sciences, 7,* 269–315.

Sternberg, R.J. (Ed.). (1984b). *Human abilities: An information processing approach.* New York: W.H. Freeman.

Sternberg, R.J., Conway, B.E., Ketron, J.L., & Bernstein, M. (1981). People's conceptions of intelligence. *Journal of Personality and Social Psychology, 41,* 37–55.

21.

Intelligence: Revisited

Sandra Scarr
University of Virginia

Although the editors claim that "views of the nature of intelligence have evolved over the years," I am dubious. Even in 1921, most experts thought of intelligence as made up primarily of higher-order mental processes, rather than elemental sensations; the lesson of Binet versus Galton was not lost on them. Contemporary views of the *processes* involved in intelligence have indeed changed, as have our ideas about the neurological bases of intelligence, but I do not think that ideas about the nature of intelligence per se have evolved so much as shifted with the cultural tides.

What Is It?

The first question concerns "What I conceive 'intelligence' to be and by what means it can be best measured . . ." ("Intelligence and its measurement," p. 123). With the question framed this way, one is led to believe there is *an* answer. And that intelligence is indeed an "it." The question should be rephrased to reflect, in my view, that there are as many answers to the question "What is intelligence?" as there are purposes in asking it. Not all answers are compatible with what we know about the nature of intellectual processing (e.g., intelligence cannot consist of 120 independent factors or nothing but one g), but there are many useful ways to address the question, depending on the goal of the question.

One question often asked about intelligence relates to its *structure* in the psychometric sense. I am satisfied that Vernon, Jensen, Eysenck, Horn, Humphreys, and others who posit a hierarchical organization from one or two general factors to more specific skills have exhausted the interesting variance in this version of the question. The first version of the ambiguous question "What is the nature of intelligence . . . ?" has yielded quite satisfactory answers to problems of selection in educational and occupational settings, and to the correlated nature of intellectual skills, however defined.

A second version of the question "What is the nature of intelligence . . . ?" addresses the *processes* by which people gather and use information to solve problems and to acquire knowledge. Mental processes are much better studied today than in 1921, through the efforts of Sternberg and a phalanx of other talented cognitive psychologists. Theories of intellectual processing, including such concepts as meta or executive components, encoding, mapping, comparison, execution, and the like, describe *how* people go about thinking and solving problems better than do older notions of multiple associations or bonds. But understanding the processes that make up intelligent problem solving in the laboratory will not, I suspect, supplant the psychometric approach to testing acquired knowledge and problem-solving skills in real-life situations. The process approach holds out more hope, however, of remediation in intellectual retardation and of training programs to improve intellectual functioning.

A third version of the question "What is the nature of intelligence . . . ?" asks about the neurological processes underlying intelligent behavior. Vernon and Jensen (1984) have found correlations in the 0.5 to 0.6 range between processing speed on simple and complex reaction-time tasks and psychometric tests. They now have a credible body of results to indicate that speed of processing complex decisions is related to other forms of intellectual processing. At a more neurological level, Eysenck (1981) shows that the reliability of the CNS in responding to evoked potentials is related to psychometric test results. The theories of these investigators are akin to the physiological theories of Thompson, McGaugh, Best, and others on the necessity of brain for mental functions. Who could doubt it? Even if our understanding of brain and mind relationships increases dramatically, this knowledge will not supplant the usefulness of answers to the first two versions of the question.

A fourth version of the question "What is the nature of intelligence . . . ?" asks about the human species history of intellectual evolution. Although this is not of major interest to the majority of psychologists, comparative scientists, such as Jerison, Premack, and Hallowell, and primatologists, such as Jolly and Patterson, have illuminated our views of the special adaptations made possible by the human version of primate intelligence. The role of language in human cognition is of special interest. The comparative understanding of the evolution of human intelligence does not compete with the former three versions of answers to the major question.

A fifth version of the question "What is the nature of intelligence . . . ?"

focuses on the sources of individual variability in contemporary populations. I claim that those of us who appreciate the nature of human variability have hardly changed our answers at all since 1921. Human intelligence, as measured by traditional tests and by more contemporary information-processing tasks, is about 50% heritable; the remaining variance is largely due to individual experience, not common to siblings in the same family or to parents and children. Many psychologists said this in the early part of the century.

Although the data on which the answers are based are more secure now than in 1921, debate about the extent to which intelligence is environmentally molded has hardly subsided. Even in the face of evidence that intellectual skills are only modestly malleable for most children in the U.S. population (but more dramatically malleable for non-mainstream children), extremists still argue over naive behaviorist versus rigid hereditarian positions.

The more interesting version of the nature-nurture debate now focuses on the influence of developmental genetic programs on individual differences in experience (e.g., Plomin, DeFries & Loehlin, 1977; Scarr & McCartney, 1983; Wilson & Matheney, 1983). If intelligent persons generate for themselves and evoke from others more intellectually stimulating environments, then the observed correlations between features of the environment and intelligence cannot be taken as a guide to intervention strategies (see Scarr, 1980, and Scarr & Weinberg, 1978, on the intervention fallacy). Individual differences in intellectual experiences can be seen as a result of individual genetic differences, rather than as a result of arbitrarily imposed, rich or limited, opportunities. Unless their environments are notably restricted, people will encounter what they are capable of, and interested in, learning and doing.

Whence Research on Intelligence?

Because there are several versions of the major question, one can safely assume that research will continue on many fronts. It is certainly important that the brain-mind connections be better detailed. And it is important to understand better how efficient information-processing strategies can be taught to those who do not use them effectively in everyday life. But I hope that a different wave of research will emerge with different kinds of theories.

The arbitrary distinctions between social, emotional, and intellectual psychology result from our own intellectual history of faculty psychology. It is high time that we reconceived of human behavior in terms of functioning, adaptation, and considerations of how people live their everyday lives.

Sternberg (1985) has made a move in this direction; others have tried to develop concepts of social competence (e.g., Messick & Anderson, 1978; Scarr, 1981; Zigler & Trickett, 1980). Many years ago, David Wechsler spoke of intelligence as a part of personality, which for him was a broader concept of human adaptation. He understood that effective intelligence depended on far more than information-processing strategies or neurological efficiency.

To be an effective, intelligent human being requires a broader form of personal adaptation and life strategy, one that has been described in "invulnerable" children and adults: They are copers, movers, and shapers of their own environments. Surely, to understand intelligence in real-world contexts, research on intelligence must make contact with motivation, emotion, and the social requirements of ordinary people. In addition, understanding intelligence requires us to take account of the evolutionary history and variability of human adaptations. Strategies for learning one's culture and for solving life's large and small problems can take many forms, even if all of them are correlated.

REFERENCES

Anderson, S., & Messick, S. (1974). Competence in young children. *Developmental Psychology, 10,* 282–293.

Eysenck, H. (1981). *The structure and measurement of intelligence.* New York: Springer-Verlag.

Intelligence and its measurement: A symposium. (1921). *Journal of Educational Psychology, 12,* 123–147, 195–216, 271–275.

Plomin, R., DeFries, J.C., & Loehlin, J.C. (1977). Genotype-environment interaction and correlation in the analysis of human behavior. *Psychological Bulletin, 84,* 309–322.

Scarr, S. (1981). Comments on psychology, behavior genetics, and social policy from an anti-reductionist. In R.A. Kasschau & C. Coffer (Eds.), *Psychology's second century—enduring issues* (pp. 147–175). New York: Praeger.

Scarr, S. (1981). Implications for assessment and intervention strategies. *American Psychologist, 36,* 1159–1166.

Scarr, S., & Carter-Saltzman, L. (1982). Genetic differences in intelligence. In R.A. Sternberg, (Ed.), *The handbook of human intelligence* (pp. 792–896). Cambridge, MA: Cambridge University Press.

Scarr, S., & McCartney, K. (1983). How people make their own environments: A theory of genotype → environment effects. *Child Development, 54,* 424–435.

Scarr, S., & Weinberg, R.A. (1978). The influence of "family background" on intellectual attainment. *American Sociological Review, 43,* 159–177.

Sternberg, R. (1985). *Beyond I.Q.* New York: Cambridge University Press.

Vernon, P., & Jensen, A. (1984). Individual and group differences in intelligence and speed of information processing. *Personality and Individual Differences, 5,* 411–423.

Wilson, R.S., & Matheney, A.P., Jr. (1983). Mental development: Family environment and genetic influences. *Intelligence, 7,* 195–215.

Zigler, E., & Trickett, P.K. (1978). IQ, social competence, and evaulation of early childhood intervention programs. *American Psychologist, 33,* 789–798.

22.

Explaining Intelligence

Roger C. Schank
Yale University

People aren't much like computers and computers aren't (at least yet) much like people, but they do have at least one thing in common. For each, scholars keep wondering if there is any way in which we can accurately test their intelligence. We don't see articles discussing whether people can think, but we would if it weren't just a matter of faith. How do we know that people are thinking, after all? We assume it, the same way most people assume that computers are not thinking.

In an attempt to find some more objective criteria for measuring, or at least confirming, the thinking capacity of computers, researchers in Artificial Intelligence (AI) have had to address some elusive questions about the nature of intelligence in general. I believe that our concerns in AI may well apply equally to people.

The question to address in this regard, is not how to measure intelligence but how to measure understanding. In AI, we want computers to understand what we say to them. Since people already seem to possess this capability, researchers in intelligence rarely seem to worry about this issue. However, it is logically prior. That is, first you have to understand, then we can worry about how much you understood.

Understanding

Understanding, we claim, consists of processing incoming experiences in terms of the cognitive apparatus one has available. This cognitive apparatus has a physical instantiation (the brain or hardware of the computer) and a mental instantiation (the mind or the software of the computer). When an episode is being processed, a person brings to bear the totality of his cognitive apparatus to attempt to understand it. What this means in practice is that people understand things in terms of their particular memories and experiences. Specifically, this means that people who have different goals, beliefs, expectations, and general lifestyles, will understand identical episodes quite differently. It also means that there are likely to be a great many different kinds of understanding.

What I would like to do is discuss a spectrum of understanding that will allow us to consider the issue more sensibly. Let's consider some of the points on that spectrum. At the far end of the spectrum, we have what I shall call COMPLETE EMPATHY. This is the kind of understanding that might obtain between twins, very close brothers, very old friends who know each other's every move and motivation, and other such combinations of people that rarely are found in the world.

At the opposite end of the spectrum we have the barest form of understanding, which I shall call MAKING SENSE. This is the point where events that occur in the world can be interpreted by the understander in terms of a coherent (although probably incomplete) picture of how those events came to pass.

Now let us step back for a moment. Before we complete this spectrum, it would be worthwhile to discuss both what the spectrum actually represents and what the relevance of current AI research is to this spectrum. The point of view we are taking here is that there is a spectrum that describes how an **understander** copes with events outside his control. The argument is that there exists a spectrum that describes what we call understanding. The end points of this spectrum can be loosely described as, on the one hand, the understander saying to himself, *Yes, I see what is going on here, it makes some sense to me,* and, on the other hand, his saying, *My God, that's exactly what I would have done, I know precisely how you feel.*

Consider, for example, the following situation. Imagine yourself going to a Burger King under the circumstances in which you have been to McDonald's on numerous occasions but have never before been to Burger King. You are confronted with a new situation which you must attempt to **understand.** We can say that a person has understood such an experience (i.e., he or she understands Burger King in the sense of being able to operate in it) when that person says, *Oh I see, Burger King is just like McDonald's.*

To put this another way, we might expect that at some point during your Burger King trip you might be **reminded** of McDonald's. The point here is that understanding, on any part of the spectrum of understanding mentioned above, means being reminded of the closest previously experienced phenomenon in memory and being able to use the expectations generated by that reminding to help in processing the current experience.

When we are reminded of some event or experience in the course of undergoing a different experience, this reminding behavior is not random. We are reminded of this experience because the structures we are using to process this new experience are the same structures we are using to organize memory. Thus, we cannot help but pass through the old memories while processing a new input. There are an extremely large number of such high-level memory structures. Finding the right one of these (that is, the one that is most specific to the experience at hand) is what we mean by understanding.

An important part of what we mean by understanding (some of the time, that is, for some kinds of understanding) is the creation of new knowl-edge structures in memory as a result of understanding. Such structures are created in terms of the old ones. To return to our fast food example, when Burger King reminds you of McDonald's, what you are thinking goes as follows: *Ah yes, Burger King is just like McDonald's except the waitresses wear red and yellow and you can have it your way.* A new discrimination in the structure that contains McDonald's is then made, creating a situation in which Burger King is a high-level structure that shares most, but not all, of its properties with the old McDonald's structures. The differences are significant in that they themselves may form the basis of reminding experi-ences. For example, a fried-chicken place that allowed you to choose the set of herbs and spices you wanted on the chicken might be called *the Burger King of the fast food fried chicken places.* This analogy could be drawn by entering the **have it your way discrimination** in the processing of the new input and finding that as the node most specific to the input. But clearly this could not be part of a hierarchy in which **hamburger** was one of the interesting discriminations.

In this view, then, understanding is finding the closest higher-level structure available to explain an input and creating a new memory structure for that input that is IN TERMS OF the old closely related higher level struc-ture. Understanding, then, is a process that has its basis in memory, particu-larly memory for closely related experiences accessible through reminding and expressible through analogy. Further, understanding is something whose depth will be greater the more there are available relevant personal experiences in terms of which inputs can be processed. With this definition of the nature of understanding, then, let us now return to our understanding spectrum.

The Spectrum of Understanding

Given the sense of the nature of understanding above, it seems clear that one reason why COMPLETE EMPATHY might exist would be that so many shared experiences between the individuals involved would have caused very similar memory structures to have been created. The consequence of this is that, given a set of similar goals and beliefs, new episodes would be processed in the same way. The above caveat is very important. Similar experiences, but different goals and beliefs, would still result in differing perceptions of the events, or to put it another way, in a lack of COMPLETE EMPATHY in understanding of each other's actions.

The point to be made about the understanding spectrum, then, is that the more completely that goals, beliefs, and prior experiences and memories are shared, the more complete the understanding that can take place. On the opposite end of the spectrum, MAKING SENSE involves finding out what events took place and relating them to a perception of the world that may be quite different from that in the mind of the actor in those events.

To make all this more clear, let us now consider what may well be a midpoint on the understanding spectrum. This midpoint I will label COGNITIVE UNDERSTANDING. By this I mean that while a man may be able to build an accurate model of the thought processes of a given woman (his wife, for example), he may still not really understand what her motivations, fears, needs, and so on are. That is, he lacks COMPLETE EMPATHY with her, but he still understandings a great deal about her. To claim that he doesn't understand her can only be referring to understanding in its deepest sense. Certainly, by any measure of understanding less than COMPLETE EMPATHY he could rightly claim to understand what she does and not be accused of failing the understanding test.

To make this argument more concrete, I will list below some possible examples for each of these points on the spectrum:

- MAKING SENSE
  input: news from the UPI wire
  output: a summary of a newspaper story; a translation of a speech into
    another language

- COGNITIVE UNDERSTANDING
  input: a set of stories about airplane crashes, complete with data about
    the airplanes and the circumstances
  output: a conclusion about what may have caused the crash that turns
    out to be accurate

- COMPLETE EMPATHY
  input: I was very upset by your actions last night.
  output: I thought you might have been; it was a lot like the way you
    treated me last week.
  input: But I meant you no harm.
  output: Do you remember the way your father used to treat you on

holidays when he made you call all your relatives? He meant no harm
either.

input: I see what you mean.

output: I thought you might; there's no friend like an old friend.

Assuming that these examples are not entirely fanciful, I would now like
to draw some conclusions about them that are reflective of my view of what
a reasonable intelligence test should comprise. My conclusions are effectively summarized with the following words:

Accuracy; Surprise; Emotion

The claim I am making is that, to the extent that output is an effective way of
characterizing degree of understanding (although that is to a very limited
extent; indeed, it may well be our only choice), we can judge the significance of that output in terms of its place on the understanding spectrum
with respect to the following features:

- The extent to which that output accurately accomplishes the task that an
  individual has set out to do.
- The extent to which that output characterizes an especially original or
  important result that most people cannot easily accomplish.
- The extent to which that output reflects a change in an individual as a
  result of his or her processing the input.

The Explanation Test

In the end, any system, human or mechanical, is judged on its output. We do
not take apart humans to look at their insides in an effort to establish that
their understanding mechanisms are of the right sort. Nor is it clear what
the right sort of mechanisms are. We are faced with a dilemma then. We
cannot use output to tell us if a system *really understands*. On the other
hand, output is all we can reasonably expect to get.

I wish to claim that the fundamental difference between a system that
can produce reasonable output and one that meets the criterion that we
mean by the label **understanding system** is that an understanding system
should be able to explain its own actions. A system that not only does
interesting things, but can explain why it did them by relating what it did to
other episodes and circumstances in its world, can be said to **understand**
at any point on the understanding spectrum where that explanation is sufficient. (This is not to say that a system that cannot explain cannot therefore
understand. The question is how an understanding system can show an

outside observer that it has understood. Humans are happy to attribute understanding capabilities to everything from cats to dolphins. Somehow, however, machines fail to enjoy such largess. So while we cannot claim that if you cannot explain you have not understood, we can claim that if you can explain you must have understood.) This criterion applies equally well to people. That is, their intelligence is linked to their ability to understand, and reflect upon, their own processes.

To make this more concrete, consider the three points on the spectrum that we have discussed. To satisfy understanding requirements at the MAKING SENSE level, acting *robot-like* will do. We need only know that the reason we did something was to enable the next event that depended upon it. Programs that act this way, for example, Winograd's SHRDLU (Winograd, 1972), tend to be fairly impressive. SHRDLU could explain that it had done X to do Y in order to do Z, and so on. At the end of its chain of reasoning, it had only the initial command given by the user. In that case, it would respond, *I did that because you asked me to.* This latter response became well-known and was psychologically very appealing. (For example, Restak, 1979, used the phrase *because you asked me to* as the title of a chapter in his popular book on the brain. That chapter was on various aspects of AI and only touched upon Winograd's work.) Although it was not put this way at the time, one of the reasons why Winograd's program was much appreciated was because it **understood** at the MAKING SENSE level on the understanding spectrum. It understood its world of blocks as well as a human would. It might be considered as having passed the Explanation Test at the level of MAKING SENSE, the criterion of which is: People can be said to understand at that level when they take reading comprehension tests. They don't read, during those tests, to assimilate new information, or to empathize with the characters. They read in order to answer questions. The stories have no real context and thus no serious explanation is required. It is important to be able to make sense of the world, of course, but differing degrees of ability in that regard may be more a test of an ability to cope in an artificially constrained situation than a test of intellectual ability.

Each point on the understanding spectrum has essentially the same requirements in the Explanation Test. For COGNITIVE UNDERSTANDING, an understander must be able to explain why it came to the conclusions it did, what hypotheses it rejected and why, how previous experiences influenced it to come up with its hypotheses, and so on. People who come up with innovative ideas, generalizations, correlations, and so on, are usually expected to explain and justify those ideas. An understander must be able to answer the question *How do you know?* Grading satisfactory explanations may prove to be a fairly difficult task, but constructing such explanations is an important facet of intelligence.

The last point we have presented on our spectrum, that of COMPLETE

EMPATHY, has no easier test. Machines may never have undergone enough experiences, nor reacted to them in the same way that people do, to satisfy people that they *really understand.* And indeed, it is probably impossible to test to see if people have understood at that level either.

It was suggested (Riesbeck, personal communication) that one way to make the distinction between passing the Explanation Test at each level is to use the example of a joke. An understander that simply understood the joke, in that it could explain what had happened, would be understanding at the level of MAKING SENSE. A system that actually found the joke funny, to the extent that it could explain what expectations had been violated, what other jokes it knew that were like it that it was reminded of, and so on, would be understanding at the level of COGNITIVE UNDERSTANDING. Finally, a being that belly-laughed because of how that joke related to its own particular experiences and really expressed a point of view about life that the program was only now realizing, would have understood at the level of COMPLETE EMPATHY.

Levels of Explanation

The key question, then, is how we are to differentiate the various kinds of explanation that are required to demonstrate understanding, be it human or computer understanding. In other words, what does it take to pass the explanation test? How can we know if we have moved from left to right on the understanding spectrum?

In this section, we shall consider how the test of explanation is to be made. The test should hopefully not merely be some ad hoc device. Rather, the explanations we seek should already be inherent in any program that purports to understand. We shall also consider what explanation tells us about intelligence, which is, I claim, the true subject matter of AI.

Bear in mind that explanation is different depending upon the point in the understanding spectrum that we are dealing with. At each point, some type of explanation is required. It is the depth and type of the explanation that varies. We expect, when hearing of an event that we wish to make sense of, to be able to put the pieces together in a whole. Thus, if we hear an account of an event, we listen to see if each element in the event relates to its parts. When it does not, we attempt to make inferences that tie together the individual elements. When we cannot make such inferences, either one of two things is the case. We may have a situation where there exists an appropriate knowledge structure that, if known, would tie together the seemingly unrelated pieces. If we do not know this structure, then we can ask about it, or attempt to discover it for ourselves. On the other hand, it may be the case that this structure does not exist. In that case, we usually say that what we heard didn't *make sense.*

Both computers and people require, for the most minimal level of understanding, a set of information that they can rely upon to tie together elements in an event that are connected but whose connection has not been explicitly stated. Thus, the first type of explanation it is important to recognize is COHERENCY EXPLANATIONS, that is, the type of explanation that relies upon a store of knowledge to draw inferences that create connectivity in a text, scene, or plan.

A second type of explanation, corresponding to the level of COGNITIVE UNDERSTANDING, is that of FAILURE EXPLANATIONS. The premise of COGNITIVE UNDERSTANDING is basically that an input, after being processed to see if all of its pieces are connected, must be processed in such a way as to relate it to previously stored experiences that a system has already processed. The process of doing this was outlined in Schank (1982). The premise there was that when an input fails to conform to expectations derived from prior experience, its differences are noted and stored. In order to achieve real insights into why an input did not match one's expectations, one must attempt to explain the failure. This explanation is then used as an index to that particular experience. When another experience fails an expectation and is explained the same way, people, and hence we must attempt to make this the case with machines, get REMINDED. This reminding serves as the basis of learning (as discussed in Schank, 1982). People learn by comparing experiences that differed from expectations in the same way, so as to enable the creation of a new set of expectations that capture the generalizations created by similar failures with similar explanations.

Thus, the first critical role of explanation is simply the tying together of events in such a way as to fill in the missing pieces so as to make sure that a smooth chain of causality exists. If this chain of causally linked events can be created, then we can argue that a system has understood, at the MAKING SENSE level.

The second level of explanation implies a deeper level of understanding. Explaining failures implies the ability to understand by relating a set of events to one's own personal experiences, since failures are by definition violations of expectations derived from one's own experience. Relating information being processed to prior information that was already processed is a qualitatively different kind of understanding. Explaining at that level is the basis of learning and thus the basis of a system that can be surprising in some sense. Thus, COGNITIVE UNDERSTANDING implies learning, and thus, in a limited sense, some elements of creativity.

It is this explanation at the cognitive understanding level that really is the hallmark of our intellectual capacities. Having a powerful memory, rich with experiences and cleverly indexed, is at the base of intelligence. Being able to recover from failed expectations by recalling prior similar experiences, and being able to learn from the comparison of the current failure to a prior experience, is what intelligence, in its richest form, is all about. Creativity, insight, and originality of expression, all depend upon our ability to recall seemingly unrelated memories and draw lessons from them to help in our current situation.

The third level, COMPLETE EMPATHY, also has connected to it a level of explanation. Often, when we hear somebody tell us about his or her daily problems, we respond with anecdotes based upon our own experiences. But there is a deeper level of understanding of another individual that is possible, and that is one that is based on a fairly sophisticated model of that individual that we have built up over time. As we get to know someone, we can build up a model of that person that explains why he acts the way he does and that predicts, to some degree, his future behavior. In a sense, the notion of COMPLETE EMPATHY that we have suggested is just the end point on a rather wide spectrum that encompasses understanding of this kind. The more we know about another human being, the more we are able to understand him. (There is that old saying that before criticizing someone you should first walk a mile in his shoes.)

The third type of explanation is what I shall call CONTRIBUTORY EXPLANATION. Here, what we are seeking is an understanding of the reasons behind an action that someone takes. When Weizenbaum's ELIZA program (Weizenbaum, 1966) responded to its **patient** that her boyfriend and her father and bullies were all intertwined, it was that response that made people believe that was something to whatever it was that Weizenbaum had done. People were impressed because there was a CONTRIBUTORY EXPLANATION. Now, in this case, what we really had was a **gimmick** that was in no way generalizable. But if it had been done by a method that was based on a theory of how such connections can be made in understanding the rationale behind the behavior of a patient, then we would have been witness to an impressive piece of work.

Intelligence

The real intent of Artificial Intelligence is, I claim, to find out what intelligence is all about. We tend to say that a person is intelligent to the extent that he or she is insightful, creative, and in general, able to relate apparently unrelated pieces of information to come up with a new way of looking at things. We tend to claim that a person is unintelligent to the extent that his or her behavior is thoroughly predictable with reference to what we know that the person knows. Thus, when someone does things the way he or she was told to do them, never questioning and thus never creating new methods, we tend to see that person as unintelligent.

I mention this here because I see the Explanation Test as a kind of intelligence test. We are not asking the computer simply to replicate intelligent behavior because we have no knowledge of which aspects of such behavior are more intelligent than others. Is composing a sonnet a more or less intelligent act than playing chess? There is no way to answer this objectively because it isn't the acts themselves that are at issue here, but rather the quality of those acts.

We can fairly easily make a program write bad sonnets or play poor chess. Neither of these feats seems much of a mark of intelligence. Indeed, working on either of them would not be considered AI any more, although such work might have seemed all right not so long ago. Today, work on computer poetry or computer chess falls within the domain of AI to the extent that it mimics the complex cognitive processes associated with the CREATIVITY inherent in both acts. Thus, if the computer poetry program started with a set of feelings and was able, by relating such feelings to its personal experiences, to create poetry, particularly poetry of some new type, we would be legitimately impressed. Similarly, if our computer chess program was capable of improving its playing ability by inventing a new strategy or employing an old one that it recalled having seen in a match it knew about, that would be an AI-type feat.

We have come to understand, in AI, that it isn't the tasks themselves that are interesting. What matters is how they are done. Thus, I claim, the only way to know if our machines, or people, are intelligent, is to make them explain how they did what they did.

Furthermore, those explanations should have some connection with how the task in question actually was performed. Often, this is a difficult task for people to perform. We do not always know where our creative powers come from or how they were employed in any given instance. But people can attempt to give rational explanations, and ultimately that is how we must measure their intelligence. Of course, under this view, their intelligence might change radically over time. Of course, if I believed that one could not change the intelligence of a being over time, I could not possibly work on making machines intelligent.

How do we grade explanations or the ability to recall relevant memories? I leave that decision to those interested in such matters. Underlying the attempt to test intelligence in a rigorous way, one would expect to find some assessment of an individual's ability to self-reflect. At the heart of that ability is the interest, desire, intelligence, or whatever it takes to generate a question. Needing to know, and trying to find out, is what makes us intelligent. I will be satisfied that computers are intelligent when one of them asks me a question that it was wondering about and that it was in no way directed to ask. Maybe, in order to test the intelligence of people, testees should be asking us the questions, instead of the other way around.

REFERENCES

Restak, R.M. (1979). *The brain: The last frontier.* Garden City, NY: Doubleday.

Schank, R.C. (1982). *Dynamic memory: A theory of learning in computers and people.* Cambridge, England: Cambridge University Press.

Weizenbaum, J. (1966). ELIZA—A computer program for the study of natural language communications between man and machine. *Communications of the Association for Computing Machinery, 9*(1), 36–45.

Winograd, T. (1972). *Understanding natural language.* New York: Academic Press.

23.

On Intelligence

Richard E. Snow
Stanford University

Definition

Definitions are rarely definitive in science. But their requirement forces conceptual concision—sometimes even excision—upon theorists. And a collection of brief definitions may be more useful for new research than a like number of books; most researchers do not incorporate that much detail into their daily thinking anyway. Implied here is the first aspect of my definition of intelligence: the incorporation of concisely organized prior knowledge into purposive thinking—for short, call it *knowledge-based thinking*.

In 1921, psychology was nearing the first high point of its apprehension of the analysis of intelligence via mental tests, so a call for definitions was appropriate. In 1986, psychology is nearing the first high point of its apprehension of the analysis of intelligence via information-processing experiments, so again the call is timely. The term *apprehension* captures the second aspect of my definition—it refers to Spearman's (1923, 1927) principle that persons (including psychologists) not only feel, strive, and know,

This chapter was written while the author served as Liaison Scientist for Psychology, Office of Naval Research–London Branch. The thinking and research on which it is based was supported by Contract N00014-79-C-0171 from the Office of Naval Research, by a James McKeen Cattell Fund award, and by a Guggenheim Fellowship award. The views and conclusions contained in this document are those of the author and should not be interpreted as necessarily representing the official policies, either expressed or implied, of the Office of Naval Research or the U.S. Government.

but also *know* that they feel, strive, and know, and can anticipate further feeling, striving, and knowing; they monitor and reflect upon their own experience, knowledge, and mental functioning in past, present, and future tenses.

Most prior definitions of intelligence (see, e.g., "Intelligence and Its Measurement," 1921; Snow, 1978) emphasize adaptive cognitive functioning, or more specifically, adaptation to changing circumstances in the service of perseverance toward an accepted goal. This is the third aspect of intelligence—*adaptive purposeful striving*. It includes the notion that one can adopt or shift strategies in performance to use what strengths one has in order to compensate for one's weaknesses.

A fourth aspect, also included in virtually all definitions of intelligence, is agile, analytic reasoning of the sort that enables significant features and dimensions of problems, circumstances, and goals to be decontextualized, abstracted, and interrelated rationally. One could elaborate the infrastructure of this aspect—called here *fluid-analytic reasoning*—using Spearman's (1927) eduction principles or the current models of Johnson-Laird (1983), Pellegrino and Glaser (1982), or Sternberg (1984), among others.

A fifth aspect is *mental playfulness*. Nature is often ambiguous; well-defined goals and problems are often not given. One needs therefore to be able to find or create interesting problems to solve and interesting goals toward which to strive. This involves both tolerance of ambiguity and pursuit of novelty—Thurstone (1924) came close in discussing inhibition of impulse and the imaginal hunt, respectively. Most importantly, one must suspend reasoning, though not apprehension, in order to explore alternative ideas, strategies, and purposes (March & Olsen, 1976; Snow, 1980).

A sixth aspect is *idiosyncratic learning*. Psychologists who study intelligence (or learning) with the assumption that the same process model fits all persons, or all items, trials, or task variations within a person, seem to deny their own apprehensions of individuality. Persons differ from one another in the way they assemble their learning and problem-solving performance, though they may achieve the same score. Persons differ *within* themselves in how they solve parts of a problem, or different problems in a series (Bethell-Fox, Lohman, & Snow, 1984; Kyllonen, Lohman, & Woltz, 1984; Snow, 1981). It appears that adaptive learning, reassembly, and strategy shifting occur within persons and within tests (or tasks). It may also be that sources of apparent unreliability in intelligence tests differ at different levels of intelligence; reliability may appear to decrease as one goes up the scale of intelligence, because of increasing idiosyncrasy.

I propose these six as among the most important aspects for a definition, but they do not together constitute a necessary and sufficient definition. I agree with Neisser (1979) that intelligence is a "family resemblance" concept. Thus the six are called "aspects" here; they are not "features" or "facets" of intelligence in the usual sense of those terms. Consider three further points.

First, the six are subtly interdependent in an organization that seems both Gestalt-like and shifty. Apprehension is often an essential part of knowledge-based thinking, and vice versa, but not always. Adaptation often requires fluid-analytic reasoning, and vice versa, but not always. Mental play and reasoning are complements, but knowing when to shift between them—apprehension?—may sometimes be critical, though not always. Mental play produces novelty, idiosyncratic learning strives for it, but knowledge-based thinking runs through both, though not always. One can go on comparing aspects in all possible pairs, triples, and so on; none seem either orthogonal, always correlated, or always present.

Second, intelligence seems to be neither a unity, as Anderson (1983) or Spearman (1923) would have it, nor a specifiable number of modules, as Fodor (1983), Gardner (1983), or Guilford (1967) would have it. One can add to my list many further proposed aspects to account for performance in particular situations. *Spatial visualization when appropriate* would likely be added next; it is usually found to be distinct as a higher-order factor (see Gustaffson, 1984). But it is not clear to what extent such a factor represents fluid-analytic reasoning applied to spatial-figural material versus a collection of special spatial skills. *Ideational fluency* or *auditory abilities* might then be next; these also may be manifestations of aspects already listed, or special skills, or some mixture. Many narrower cognitive ability factors and mental processes displayable with special tests or laboratory tasks could be proposed. But then the list expands interminably, with diminishing return for new research, reaching a level of grain that highlights the dots in the newspaper photo and loses what the dots depict. Also, sooner or later in such a list, *speed when appropriate* and *efficient working memory,* for example, would appear. But then the list turns back on itself—these are aspects of aspects that appear earlier in the list, and perhaps reflect mechanisms that help explain individual differences in the earlier aspects; they are not themselves distinct aspects, for they are also aspects of many human performances that would not be called "intelligence."

Finally, one must list the many empirical facts that should be acknowledged in a definition, because they must be explained by a theory. But no one set of features is likely to explain them all. One major fact is that matrices of intercorrelations derived from representative samples of mental tests and persons routinely show not only positive manifold and a G factor but also an inverse Guttman Radex structure around the central G factor (Snow, Kyllonen, & Marshalek, 1984). There appears to be a continuum of increasing complexity in processing as one steps in from peripheral to central tests on any array of the radex structure. But it is not likely that the same aspects of intelligence account for increasing complexity in all regions of the radex. Two other facts are that tests in the central region of the radex usually predict complex cognitive outcomes of formal training or instruction, and often display interaction with instructional treatments that appear to differ in their demand for learning in the face of instructional incompleteness and lack of structure (Snow & Lohman, 1984). But predictive and differential validity vary across situations; again it is unlikely that the same aspects of intelligence underlie all these situational variations. Many other facts, developmental as well as differential, could also be discussed; differentiation of intelligence with age and education, for example, suggests the same problem (Anastasi, 1970).

Given all this, what kind of organizational model of human cognition can be suggested that displays observed intelligence? I think of it this way: Intelligence is an "artifact" in Simon's (1969) sense of that term; it is that part of the internal environment that shows through at the interface between person and external environment as a function of cognitive task demands. Whenever there is mismatch between task demands and person response, or task affordance and person initiative, individual differences in some aspects of intelligence show through at the interface. The inner environment can be considered a very large bank of cognitive processing components and chunks of organized knowledge from which samples are drawn according to the demands or affordances of particular outer environments. Thus, different tests or tasks may call more or less different samples, or aspects, into view; correlations between tests are measures of sampling similarity. The sampling theory of intelligence stems from Thomson (1919, 1939) as adapted by Humphreys (1971, 1979) and further adapted here. The bits and pieces of the bank can be described as S-R bonds, information-processing components, schemata, plans, learning sets, generalization tendencies, knowledge structures in semantic networks, productions in production systems, or all of these. They are loosely coupled, and idiosyncratically and probabilistically organized, so many different sorts of assemblies of them can be composed in different ways for different purposes, and readily decomposed. For familiar tasks, the relevant assembly may be over-learned, stored, and sampled, as a unit. For novel or changing tasks, considerable new assembly and adaptive reassembly may be required during performance. Certainly, individuals may differ in the contents of their banks, and in the efficiency with which particular programs or program components can be executed once assembled. But they also differ in the assembly and control functions involved in sampling at the interface. I do not claim these two functions as aspects of intelligence like the others, because I think them instrumental in the manifestation of all individual differences in aptitude, including achievement motivation and anxiety, for example. Assembly and control functions in working memory would be my candidates for "basic" mechanisms of individual differences, if there are to be any. But that is another story.

Measurement and Next Steps for Research

The assembly and control functions at the interface need to be understood in examining each of the six or more aspects of intelligence noted above. They should provide the process language by which to explain how these aspects come to be manifested through different test, task, or situation demands. They may also help explain how it is that apparently simple measures of cortical response or reaction time can correlate with complex test performance (see, e.g., Eysenck, 1982).

Some existing group tests now provide practically useful measures of analytic reasoning and knowledge-based thinking, at least for some purposes. These are the aspects most strongly reflected in tests that form the oft-obtained fluid (G_f) and crystallized (G_c) intelligence factors, respectively. Total scores on these tests may also implicitly measure adaptation and apprehension processes operating across items, though in slightly different ways in the two factors because the tests tax assembly and control operations somewhat differently. The hypothesis is that G_f represents more short-term adaptive assembly for performance on relatively novel tasks, whereas G_c represents more long-term assembly of crystallized programs retrieved as units for performance on relatively familiar tasks. But both are mixtures. New research needs to focus on the design and study of faceted tests of G_f and G_c (and also the special domain of spatial visualization, or G_v) as within-person experiments to analyze task demand theoretically and to provide diagnostic distinctions for practical use. Tasks should be chosen for this research to represent the complexity continua of the radex model. Contrasts within and between tasks should especially be chosen to isolate sources of variance associated with adaptation and apprehension processes. It is important to note that total score variance may contain effects from these sources, whereas individual item variances may not; computerized tests built only on item psychometrics may miss or distort these between-item aspects of intelligence.

The measurement of mental playfulness and idiosyncracy has hardly begun. Aside from isolated work on creativity and special individuals, there is little to go on. Hence, the research need is for broad and unfettered exploration of these phenomena, using as a base the cognitive-differential theories now in hand. On the other hand, I have given the modular view, which would equally emphasize social skills or musical ability, short shrift. Research in these areas is important in its own right, and may contribute to our understanding of assembly and control functions. But it does not illuminate the aspects of intelligence directly. I would, however, emphasize the need for research on conative and affective aspects of cognitive performance, because there is growing reason to expect subtle intersections between individual differences in motivation, volition, anxiety, and so forth, and individual differences in intellectual performance (Snow & Farr, in press). The reader may notice that my descriptions of aspects of intelligence leave room for cognitive-conative-affective interactions.

Finally, as a first next step for research, I would urge that we all reread Binet, Galton, Spearman, Thomson, and Thurstone, at least, in detail. I do not think that the modern cognitive psychology of intelligence gives them their due, or uses their rich hypotheses to guide the very broad front of research on the cognitive, conative, and affective aspects of intelligence that is needed.

REFERENCES

Anastasi, A. (1970). On the formation of psychological traits. *American Psychologist, 25,* 899–910.

Anderson, J.R. (1983). *The architecture of cognition.* Cambridge, MA: Harvard University Press.

Bethell-Fox, C.E., Lohman, D.F., & Snow, R.E. (1984). Adaptive reasoning: Componential and eye movement analysis of geometric analogy performance. *Intelligence, 8,* 205–238.

Eysenck, H.J. (Ed.). (1982). *A model for intelligence.* Berlin: Springer-Verlag.

Fodor, J.A. (1983). *The modularity of mind.* Cambridge, MA: MIT Press.

Gardner, H. (1983). *Frames of mind.* New York: Basic Books.

Guilford, J.P. (1967). *The nature of human intelligence.* New York: McGraw-Hill.

Gustaffson, J.-E. (1984). A unifying model for the structure of intellectual abilities. *Intelligence, 8,* 179–203.

Humphreys, L.G. (1971). Theory of intelligence. In R. Cancro (Ed.), *Intelligence: Genetic and environmental influences* (pp. 31–42). New York: Grune & Stratton.

Humphreys, L.G. (1979). The construct of general intelligence. *Intelligence, 3,* 105–120.

Intelligence and its measurement: A symposium. (1921). *Journal of Educational Psychology, 12,* 123–147, 195–216, 271–275.

Johnson-Laird, P.N. (1983). *Mental models.* London: Cambridge University Press.

Kyllonen, P.C., Lohman, D.F., & Woltz, D.J. (1984). Componential modeling of alternative strategies for performing spatial tasks. *Journal of Educational Psychology, 76,* 1325–1345.

March, J.G., & Olsen, J.P. (1976). *Ambiguity and choice in organizations.* Bergen, Norway: Universitetsforlaget.

Neisser, U. (1979). The concept of intelligence. *Intelligence, 3,* 217–227.

Pellegrino, J.W., & Glaser, R. (1982). Analyzing aptitudes for learning: Inductive reasoning. In R. Glaser (Ed.), *Advances in instructional psychology* (Vol. 2, pp. 269–345). Hillsdale, NJ: Erlbaum.

Simon, H.A. (1969). *The sciences of the artificial.* Cambridge, MA: MIT Press.

Spearman, C. (1923). *The nature of "intelligence" and the principles of cognition.* London: Macmillan.

Spearman, C. (1927). *The abilities of man.* London: Macmillan.

Snow, R.E. (1978). Theory and method for research on aptitude processes. *Intelligence, 2,* 225–278.

Snow, R.E. (1980). Intelligence for the year 2001. *Intelligence, 4,* 185–199.

Snow, R.E. (1981). Toward a theory of aptitude for learning I. Fluid and crystallized abilities and their correlates. In M.P. Friedman, J.P. Das, & N. O'Connor (Eds.), *Intelligence and learning* (pp. 345–362). New York: Plenum.

Snow, R.E., & Farr, M.J. (Eds.). (in press). *Aptitude, learning, and Instruction: Vol. 3. Conative and affective process analyses.* Hillsdale, NJ: Erlbaum.

Snow, R.E., Kyllonen, P.C., and Marshalek, B. (1984). The topography of ability and learning correlations. In R.J. Sternberg (Ed.), *Advances in the psychology of human intelligence* (Vol. 2, pp. 47–103). Hillsdale, NJ: Erlbaum.

Snow, R.E., & Lohman, D.F. (1984). Toward a theory of cognitive aptitude for learning from instruction. *Journal of Educational Psychology, 76,* 347–376.

Sternberg, R.J. (1984). Toward a triarchic theory of human intelligence. *The Behavioral and Brain Sciences, 7,* 269–315.

Thomson, G.H. (1919). On the cause of hierarchical order among the correlation coefficients of a number of variates taken in pairs. *Proceedings of the Royal Society, Series A, 95,* 400–408.

Thomson, G.H. (1939). *The factorial analysis of human ability.* London: University of London Press.

Thurstone, L.L. (1924). *The nature of intelligence.* Westport, CT: Greenwood Press.

24.

Intelligence Is Mental Self-Government

Robert J. Sternberg

Yale University

Intelligence is mental self-government. It can be understood, in part, by elaboration of the analogy between intelligence, on the one hand, and the nature of government, on the other. The essence of intelligence is that it provides a means to govern ourselves so that our thoughts and actions are organized, coherent, and responsive to both our internally driven needs and to the needs of the environment. Thus, intelligence may be seen as doing for the individual what a government does for individuals in collectivity. Indeed, we may have subconsciously created our styles of government, and the theories underlying them, so as to provide a mirror of the mind of man. Many of the properties that pertain to government pertain as well to intelligence, but some forms of intelligence, like some forms of government, simply do not work. A theory of intelligence that proposes a form of mental self-government that simply cannot work is likely to be incomplete, at best, and wrong, at worst. The theory of government may be useful in pointing out such inadequate theories.

Let us pursue, for the moment, the model of intelligence as mental self-government, and elaborate the kinds of questions and answers the model provides about the nature and function of intelligence. This set of questions and answers will serve as a basis for evaluating the validity and heuristic usefulness of the model.

Functions of Government

Governments can serve a number of functions, but surely, three of the main ones are to legislate, to execute, and to judge or evaluate. In the United

States, we have three branches of government to accomplish these functions: the legislative, the executive, and the judiciary. The three branches of government provide a system of checks and balances for each other. Although different nations, both present and past, have organized these three branches of government in different ways, all three functions have always been served in some form or another.

So it is with the mind. Intelligence must legislate, execute, and evaluate. This fact has been recognized in most modern theories of intelligence. Indeed, the distinction between cognition and metacognition is useful largely because it provides a convenient way of distinguishing legislative and judicial functions, on the one hand, from executive ones, on the other (cf. Brown & DeLoache, 1978). Contextual theorists such as Berry (1974), Goodnow (1976), and Neisser (1979) have recognized the role of society as well as of the individual in carrying out the three functions of government.

Levels of Government

The Hierarchical Nature of the Levels

Governments are almost inevitably hierarchical in nature, whether or not the levels of the hierarchy are explicitly defined. The names and often the functions of the various levels of the hierarchy differ from one nation to another, and from one period of history to another, but the functions described above are served—often with some redundancy—at multiple levels of government. In the United States, we have federal, state, and local levels. In certain other governments, provinces or departments might be substituted for what we call states. But the hierarchical organization remains.

Similarly, intelligence is hierarchically organized. In recent years, this simple fact has been recognized by theorists from virtually all schools of thought, including the psychometric (e.g., Cattell, 1971; Horn, 1968; Humphreys, 1962; Vernon, 1971), the cognitive (e.g., Brown, 1978; Snow, 1979; Sternberg, 1979), and the Piagetian (Piaget, 1972). Diverse theorists conceptualize the hierarchies in somewhat different ways, and with somewhat different units of analysis. But some form of hierarchy is nevertheless proposed. Nonhierarchical forms of government do not seem to work well, and neither would a nonhierarchical form of intelligence.

The Partitions of the Levels

Wherever there are multiple units at a given level of government, the multiple units must be partitioned in some way, usually geographically. For example, at the state level, the United States has 50 distinctive units; at the local level, it has many more cities and towns, and even more communities within these cities and towns. Two important facts about these partitionings must be recognized. First, the fineness of partitioning depends upon one's particular purposes. The country can be divided into states and the states into cities and the cities into communities and the communities into zones, and so on. The fineness of the partitioning one wishes to address will depend upon the purposes for which it is addressed. Second, even the nature of the partitioning will depend upon one's particular purposes. In understanding the functioning of government in the United States, the hierarchy of states, cities, and districts represents only one possible partitioning of the country. One could also partition the country in terms of population (different policies are needed, say, for dealing with sparsely populated rural areas as opposed to heavily populated cities), land use (different policies are needed, say, for farmland as opposed to industrial settings), or climate (the kinds of decisions that need to be made in areas where heavy snow is a problem are different from those that need to be made where it hardly ever snows at all), to name just a few of the possible partitionings.

There is no one right organization or level of organization, either of government or of intelligence. Each of these constructs is organized in multiple ways, and the organization of interest will depend upon the purposes for which one wishes to understand that organization. This is not to say that any organization at all is possible or correct, but merely to say that there are, within the limits of truth about government or intelligence, multiple possible organizations and levels of organization.

Forms of Government

The recognition of an analogy between forms of government and intelligence, like so much else in the field of intelligence, can be traced back to Spearman (1927). Spearman realized that different models of intelligence could be analogized to different forms of government, such as monarchy, oligarchy, and anarchy. A monarchic model, for example, would propose that there is a ruling g, or general factor, in intelligence, and not much else of consequence. An oligarchic model would propose a small number of mental abilities working together to govern the individual's thoughts and actions. An anarchic model would propose multiple elements of intelligence without any clear organization or system for getting things done.

My own triarchic theory (Sternberg, 1985) would probably best be characterized as a modified, federated oligarchy. Obviously, the modified federated oligarchy is not the only form of government that might comprise intelligent mental functioning. But it is important to keep in mind that not all governmental systems work equally well, and that the problems of various governmental systems for collectivities can apply as well to individuals. Historically, anarchies have not worked very well in practice, and have tended fairly rapidly to be supplanted by more organized forms of government. Similarly, I doubt that an anarchic mind could function very successfully in producing intelligent thought or behavior over any extended period of time. Dictatorships can be unusually efficient in accomplishing certain ends, but tend to lack the flexibility that is needed to survive over the long haul; and flexibility is a hallmark of an intelligent mind (Campione & Brown, 1979), just as it is a hallmark of an intelligent government of state. In comparing alternative models of mental self-government, therefore, one might wish to look to their overall success, as well as to their particular strengths and limitations, when these models have been implemented at the societal level.

It is important to recognize the existence of individual differences in forms of mental self-government, just as there are differences in forms of government for the nations of the world, both past and present. Some individuals do actually seem to have less organized minds than others; similarly, some people seem to be driven in their functioning by a smaller number of abilities than others. This is not to say that certain people are totally lacking in various abilities, but rather that they do not necessarily draw upon as wide a range of abilities in their mental self-government. As a result, they may miss opportunities that would be available if they were more flexible in the abilities they were willing to bring to bear upon the problems they confront. In short, there may be no single model of mental self-government that precisely characterizes all individuals. Between and even within general classes of models, there may be considerable interindividual variation.

Scope of Government

People, like states, must deal both with external or foreign affairs—their relations with other self-governments—and with internal or domestic affairs—their relations to themselves. Neither domain can be understood, or efficaciously addressed, in isolation from the other. From the governmental point of view, therefore, it is curious to find theorists of intelligence who argue either that intelligence can be understood solely as a cognitive phenomenon within the individual (e.g., Jensen, 1979) or that intelligence can be understood solely as a social phenomenon within the culture (e.g., Berry, 1974). As many contemporary theorists of intelligence have recognized (e.g., Valsiner, 1984; see also contributors in this volume), intelligence must be understood in terms of the interaction of the individual with the environment, including its social aspect.

Quite simply, intelligence must be viewed in the contexts to which it is applied. There exists a cognitive system independent of the environment. It is the goal of theories of cognition to specify what that cognitive system is, and how it works. But the goal of a theory of intelligence goes beyond specification of the cognitive system. It includes the specification of a cognitive system in a way that is valued in one or more contexts, and hence labeled "intelligent." Intelligence, like government, involves aspects both of discovery and of invention. There exists a cognitive system the nature of which needs to be discovered. But the manifestations of this cognitive system that are labeled intelligence in a given culture or society are an invention of that culture or society, and the inventive aspect of intelligence must be recognized as well as its discovered aspect. For example, "identifying important problems," as a cognitive operation, is probably a part of intelligence in all societies, and in all mental self-governments. But what problems are considered important will vary across societies. On the one hand, we wish to understand how people identify important problems. On the other hand, we also wish to understand what problems are considered important. Without understanding both of these aspects of intelligence, we are susceptible to conceptualizing intelligence in ways that are appropriate in one culture but not in another: The problems that one society might consider as important bases for distinguishing the intelligent from the unintelligent might be viewed as trivial bases for the distinction in another society. Typical IQ tests, for example, have this very property of being considered of differential merit across societies.

The Political Spectrum in Government

Governments are commonly dubbed as right-wing, left-wing, or something in between. At the same time, people recognize that no single dimension captures all of the nuances of differences in government policy, and that no single point, even in a multidimensional space, adequately captures the range of policies a given government is likely to condone. A government may be liberal in domestic policy but conservative in foreign policy, or it may be liberal in some aspects of domestic policy but not in others.

Mental self-governments have these same complexities. Individuals differ in their degrees of mental conservatism and liberalism, both between and within individuals. In other words, individuals who adopt a conservative style in the solution of one problem may adopt a more liberal style in the solution of another problem, and vice versa. By a conservative style, I refer to a style that emphasizes past methods and styles of solution in the present. By a liberal style, I refer to a style that departs more from the past.

In Piagetian terms, one might view "assimilation" as essentially a conservative style—one understands new information in terms of existing cognitive structures—and "accommodation" as essentially a liberal style—one creates new cognitive structures to understand new information. The essential things to note here are first that conservatism and liberalism are styles—it is not the case that one style is better or worse independent of the situation in which the style is used—and second, that some aspects of both styles are needed across problem situations. The style needs to be tailored to the problem situation. The same can probably be said of government: It needs to be flexible enough both to assimilate new information to existing structures when necessary, and to accommodate new information when existing policies and practices do not set a clear precedent for how a new situation should be handled.

To put things in somewhat different terms, Sternberg and Hunt (in preparation) contrast the roles of what they believe to be two fundamental modes of dealing with problems: flexibility and proceduralization. Flexibility refers to the ability to handle new problems in ways that may differ from those that have been characteristic of past performance (the liberal style). Proceduralization refers to the bringing to bear of past processes and strategies for solving problems to new problems (the conservative style). Intelligence, according to Sternberg and Hunt, represents the balance between flexibility and proceduralization, or in political terms, between liberalism and conservatism.

Efficacy of Government

The above discussion points to a critical feature that I believe applies to both governments of collectivities and mental self-governments. There is no one criterion for evaluating governments, and there is no one dependent measure that captures the essence of how well a government is succeeding. The same applies for mental self-government. There simply is no one criterion for the quality of intelligence.

In the field of intelligence, there has historically been a push toward identifying a single criterion on the basis of which to evaluate a person's intelligence. This criterion might be IQ, or mental speed, or mental power, or EEG pattern. This striving toward simplification is understandable: The goal of a science of behavior, as of a science of anything else, is to be reductionist—to understand a complex phenomenon in simple terms. But there is a danger in being overly reductionist: In striving to find a single dependent variable that adequately captures the complexity of a phenomenon, one can lose the phenomenon, or reduce it to something manageable that bears only the vaguest resemblance to the phenomenon in all its richness.

If one looks at intelligence in all its richness and diversity, it becomes literally impossible to capture its essence in any single dependent variable. Sometimes, of course, it makes sense to be fast: If one is taking an intelligence test, or performing cognitive tasks in the laboratory, perhaps the best strategy is indeed to solve problems rapidly. But there are any number of situations in life where the intelligent course of action requires reflection and holding back of one's instinctive responses (cf. Stenhouse, 1973; Thurstone, 1924). An overly rapid decision to a problem can lead to a decision that represents a satisficing rather than an optimizing strategy (Simon, 1957). One may pass up the best solution to a problem in one's haste to propose any solution at all.

Intelligence, like government, must be judged in terms of a diversity of criteria. In the triarchic theory (Sternberg, 1985), speed of component execution, accuracy of component execution, ability to deal with novelty, ability to automatize information processing, and ability to bring the components of intelligence to bear upon practical situations are all different aspects of intelligence. No one is likely to be extremely good or extremely bad in all of these aspects of problem solving. What is of interest is the profile of intelligence rather than any single score that, in summarizing all of this information, obscures the interesting patterns in it. Efficacy of mental self-government, like efficacy of political governments, is multiply produced, and must be multiply understood and measured.

REFERENCES

Berry, J.W. (1974). Radical cultural relativism and the concept of intelligence. In J.W. Berry & P.R. Dasen (Eds.), *Culture and cognition: Readings in cross-cultural psychology* (pp. 225–229). London: Methuen.

Brown, A.L. (1978). Knowing when, where, and how to remember: A problem of metacognition. In R. Glaser (Ed.), *Advances in instructional psychology* (Vol. 1, pp, 77–165). Hillsdale, NJ: Erlbaum.

Brown, A.L., & DeLoache, J.S. (1978). Skills, plans, and self-regulation. In R. Siegler (Ed.), *Children's thinking: What develops?* (pp. 3–35). Hillsdale, NJ: Erlbaum.

Campione, J.C., & Brown, A.L. (1979). Toward a theory of intelligence: Contributions from research with retarded children. In R.J. Sternberg and D.K. Detterman (Eds.), *Human intelligence: Perspectives on its theory and measurement* (pp. 139–164). Norwood, NJ: Ablex.

Cattell, R.B. (1971). *Abilities: Their structure, growth and action.* Boston, MA: Houghton Mifflin.

Goodnow, J.J. (1976). The nature of intelligent behavior: Questions raised by cross-cultural studies. In L.B. Resnick (Ed.), *The nature of intelligence* (pp. 169–188). Hillsdale, NJ: Erlbaum.

Horn, J.L. (1968). Organization of abilities and the development of intelligence. *Psychological Review, 75*, 242–259.

Humphreys, L.G. (1962). The organization of human abilities. *American Psychologist, 17*, 475–483.

Jensen, A.R. (1979). g: Outmoded theory or unconquered frontier? *Creative Science and Technology, 2,* 16–29.

Neisser, U. (1979). The concept of intelligence. *Intelligence, 3,* 217–227.

Piaget, J. (1972). *The psychology of intelligence.* Totowa, NJ: Littlefield, Adams.

Simon, H.A. (1957). *Administrative behavior* (2nd ed.). New York: Macmillan.

Snow, R.E. (1979). Theory and method for research on aptitude process. In R.J. Sternberg & D.K. Detterman (Eds.), *Human intelligence: Perspectives on its theory and measurement* (pp. 105–137). Norwood, NJ: Ablex.

Spearman, C. (1927). *The abilities of man.* New York: Macmillan.

Stenhouse, D. (1973). *The evolution of intelligence: A general theory and some of its implications.* New York: Harper & Row.

Sternberg, R.J. (1979). The nature of mental abilities. *American Psychologist, 34,* 214–230.

Sternberg, R.J. (1985). *Beyond IQ: A triarchic theory of human intelligence.* New York: Cambridge University Press.

Sternberg, R.J., & Hunt, E.B. (in preparation). *Flexibility, proceduralization, and intelligence.*

Thurstone, L.L. (1924). *The nature of intelligence.* New York: Harcourt, Brace.

Valsiner, J. (1984). Conceptualizing intelligence: From an internal static attribution to the study of the process structure of organism-environment relationships. In P.S. Fry (Ed.), *Changing conceptions of intelligence and intellectual functioning: Current theory and research* (pp. 63–89). New York: North-Holland.

Vernon, P.E. (1971). *The structure of human abilities.* London: Methuen.

25.

Intelligence: A Developmental Approach

Edward Zigler
Yale University

Throughout my work I have emphasized the arbitrary nature of definitions. A definition cannot be right or wrong, only more or less useful. So it is with any definition of intelligence. Some consensus can probably be found for the view that intelligence is a hypothetical construct referring to an individual's cognitive processes. Given this, the issue remains of whether intelligence represents a single cognitive process, or a variety of relatively discrete cognitive processes which could be individually sampled and summed to yield a comprehensive assessment of intelligence.

My view of intelligence is similar to Piaget and Werner's, insofar as I am a stage theorist. I part company from them, however, on two basic issues. First, my approach to intelligence places more emphasis on the role of experience than those of the traditional stage theorists. An environmentalist may accept Piaget's rubric since it describes experience as influencing maturation by revealing latent gaps and contradictions in mental schemas and thus acting as a catalyst for reorganization. Yet as serious students of Piaget note (Hunt, 1961; Wolff, 1960) little in his theory addresses the effects of environmental variation on individual differences in intellectual functioning.

Thus I take issue with Piaget's cognitive-developmental approach, which defines only the normative mind to the exclusion of individual variation. As has been stated (Martin, 1959; Zigler, 1963), Piaget is more of an epistemologist than a psychologist. Where Piaget's concern is the modal, mine is with individual difference.

My definition of intelligence is most similar to the polygenic model of behavior geneticists. This group advances the only interactionist definition of intelligence, including the effects of experience as well as the biological, constitutional, and genetic characteristics of the individual.

My developmental approach to individual variation in intelligence is most simply demonstrated by Figure 1. The vertical arrow represents time's passage. Horizontal arrows represent events which effect the individual, represented by a pair of vertical lines. Cognitive development is depicted as an ascending spiral, in which the numbered loops represent successive stages of growth. The approach to cognitive development represented is essentially interactionist; experience interacts with a variety of autochthonous factors in development of the intellect. One caveat is in order regarding Figure 1. It represents only the development of the cognitive system, which is only one determinant of behavior. As will be discussed, a number of factors interact to affect behavior.

In this model, a cognitive stage represents the formal cognitive processes delineated by a number of theorists, including Piaget, Vygotsky, Werner, Luria, Bruner, Kohlberg. It is this collection of cognitive processes that constitute the intellect and is, therefore, the appropriate referent for the construct of intelligence (Zigler, 1982). In keeping with most developmental-cognitive theory, a stage in this model represents all *formal* cognitive processes (i.e., the structural features), not the specific contents of behavior or phenotypic intellectual achievements.

Any test of intelligence must address this process-content distinction. We must turn our attention from the ostensible content of tests, that is, the right or wrong answer, and instead assess the processes that determine content. Conventional tests are dismissed by process-oriented cognitive

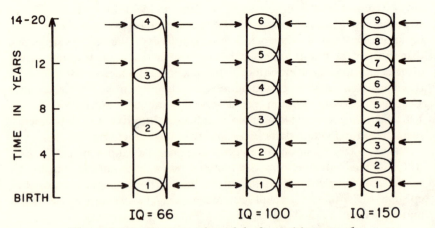

Figure 1. Developmental model of cognitive growth.

theorists for their failure to identify the salient variables of intellectual functioning:

> Their analytic and artificial character has been emphasized too often to require further reiteration. As Piaget and Inhelder, for instance, pointed out on several occasions, these tests measure only the end product of intellectual activity, but they completely disregard the internal dynamics of mental operation. One would be ill-advised to draw definite conclusions, on the basis of test results, about the quality of the reasoning process or about the fundamental nature of intellectual maturity. (Laurendeau & Pinard, 1962, p. 48)

Since Galton, psychologists have searched for a test that reveals intellectual capacity, unaffected by experience. Ertl, in an early, unsuccessful attempt, developed a "Neural Efficiency Analyzer," which he believed measured the speed of information transmission in the brain (Kimble, Garmezy, & Zigler, 1974). Eysenck's (1979) more promising approach measures the speed of neural firing. With such technological advances as gene mapping I predict we will soon realize the importance of biology in intelligence, and devise a physiological test that will identify and quantify the genotypic determinants of intelligence. Until such a test is available, however, it will be useful to recognize the elements reflected in performance on current intelligence tests. There are three such elements: (a) formal cognitive processes; (b) informational achievements, i.e. content, and (c) motivational factors (Zigler & Butterfield, 1968). Culturally deprived children may have an adequate formal cognitive storage-and-retrieval system to master the answer to the Binet vocabulary question "What is a gown?" but respond incorrectly because they have never heard the word "gown," and thus had no opportunity to learn the term. Motivational factors can also alter performance. Economically disadvantaged children, whom experience have taught to be wary, may know what a gown is, but respond "I don't know" to escape interacting with an unfamiliar and possibly dangerous adult. Much of my research has demonstrated that intervention programs such as Head Start can influence this motivational system to enable children to achieve higher scores on tests intended to evaluate formal cognitive processes and available information. The motivational component of test performance seems to be more open to experiential manipulations than are either the formal cognitive processes or informational achievements.

A valid assessment of an individual's functioning would consist of a variety of measures, including a test of formal cognitive ability (such as the standard IQ test or Piagetian model of cognitive functioning), an achievement measure (e.g., the PIAT) and some indicator of motivational and emotional variables (such as self-image or locus of control). I am aware of the measurement problems involved in assessing motivational and emotional attributes, but do not view them as insurmountable.

Finally, we must ask whether intelligence is the only or even the most useful construct to consider in assessing level of functioning. It might help to include a fourth element with those determining outcome of a test or intervention; social competence, i.e. the ability to meet societal expectations (Zigler, 1984). Many are now attempting, with a significant degree of success, to measure social competence. Again, the question is not whether a definition of intelligence is true or false, but its heuristic value. The approach outlined here has certainly been useful to me over the past quarter of a century.

REFERENCES

Eysenck, H.J. (1979). *The structure and measurement of intelligence.* New York: Springer-Verlag.

Hunt, J. (1961). *Intelligence and experience.* New York: Ronald Press.

Kimble, G., Garmezy, N.E., & Zigler, E. (1974). *Principles of general psychology* (4th ed.). New York: Ronald Press.

Laurendeau, M., & Pinard, A. (1962). *Causal thinking in the child.* New York: International University Press.

Martin, W. (1959). Rediscovering the mind of the child: A significant trend in research in child development. *Merrill-Palmer Quarterly, 6,* 67–76.

Wolff, P. (1960). The developmental psychologies of Jean Piaget and psychoanalysis. *Psychological Issues, 2* (entire).

Zigler, E. (1963). Metatheoretical issues in developmental psychology. In M. Marx (Ed.), *Theories in contemporary psychology* (pp. 341–369). New York: Macmillan.

Zigler, E. (1982). Developmental versus difference theories of mental retardation and the problem of motivation. In E. Zigler & D. Balla (Eds.), *Mental retardation: The developmental-difference controversy* (pp. 163–188). Hillsdale, NJ: Erlbaum.

Zigler, E. (1984, April). *Conceptions of social competence.* Paper presented at the Mediax Conference, Washington, DC.

Zigler, E., & Butterfield, E.C. (1968). Motivational aspects of changes in IQ test performances of culturally deprived nursery school children. *Child Development, 39,* 1–14.

PART III

INTEGRATIONS

26.

Quantitative Integration: Definitions of Intelligence: A Comparison of the 1921 and 1986 Symposia

Robert J. Sternberg
Cynthia A. Berg

Yale University

The present symposium on the definition and measurement of intelligence follows its predecessor by 65 years. How have views about intelligence developed, if at all, over the course of 65 years? The present chapter briefly addresses this question through a quantitative analysis and comparison of the present and past views of intelligence as expressed in these two symposia.

The Panel of Experts

The editors of the 1921 symposium and the present editors both sought to choose those experts of greatest renown to comment upon the definition of intelligence, and to comment upon the next steps in research. Before proceeding to an analysis of what these experts had to say, it is of interest to consider the research interests of the editors of the two symposia, the composition and nature of the journals that hosted these symposia, and the backgrounds of the experts who were asked to contribute.

In 1921 the board of editors of *The Journal of Educational Psychology* included Harold Rugg as chairman, and James Bell, Frank Freeman, Arthur Gates, Vivian Henmon, Rudolf Pintner, Beardsley Ruml, Lewis Terman, Edward Thorndike, and Laura Zirbes. All of these researchers had as their primary affiliation educational psychology, as they were all in departments of education and published extensively on issues in mental testing. Their research interests included giftedness, mental retardation, special aptitudes (e.g., art, music, and so on), and lower- and higher-order aspects of intelligence. These researchers were particularly concerned with the products of human intelligence (e.g., how well individuals performed on intelligence tests) and the utility of these products in predicting future academic and occupational performance. *The Journal of Educational Psychology,* to a certain extent a reflection of the interests of these researchers, was devoted to the investigation of problems of learning and teaching. The 1921 symposium was an outgrowth of a reorganization of *The Journal of Educational Psychology.* This reorganization was intended, in part, to provide critical papers on the use of intelligence tests.

In 1986, Robert Sternberg and Douglas Detterman have edited the current symposium. These two researchers have somewhat broader affiliations than did the editors of the 1921 symposium. Both Sternberg and Detterman are in departments of psychology, and are committed to issues of individual differences in human abilities. However, their interests extend to individual differences not only in the products of human abilities but also in the processes of mental functioning. In addition, these two researchers are interested in issues of mental retardation, the development of intelligence, the potential changing nature of intelligence across development and across cultures, the context of intelligence, and other issues within the field of cognitive psychology. The journal *Intelligence* is devoted to an understanding of the nature and function of intelligence through a multidisciplinary perspective.

In the 1921 symposium, most of the experts who were asked to contribute were educational psychologists whose main interests appear to have been in prediction of various kinds, especially of academic performance. Contributors to the 1921 symposium discussed noncognitive constructs such as will, motivation, personality, and the like, but primarily because such constructs might increase prediction of academic performance. The inclusion of experts whose backgrounds were nearly exclusively educational in nature is not surprising given the board of editors as discussed above, although psychologists outside of the field of education were also interested in the construct of intelligence (e.g., Boas—see Berry & Dasen. 1974—in cross-cultural psychology; Goddard, 1919, regarding heredity and intelligence; and several researchers in employment testing, see Hale, 1982).

In 1986, the composition of the panel of experts has changed, as we might anticipate, given the editors of this monograph. The panel includes psychologists with diverse allegiances within the field of psychology: Educational psychology is still represented, but so are cognitive psychology, cross-cultural psychology, developmental psychology, cognitive science, behavior genetics, mental retardation research, psychometrics, social psychology, and the like. These experts show less concern for prediction and more concern for understanding the scope of the construct of intelligence. To the extent that issues of prediction arise, these issues concern at least as much prediction outside the academic realm as within it.

Although the two symposia represent different samples of psychologists drawn from the larger pool of psychologists interested in intelligence (i.e., in 1921 primarily educational psychologists, in 1986 a broader range of psychologists), this differential distribution of psychologists by affiliations is itself of interest. In 1921, the construct of intelligence was more closely bound to issues of mental testing, and was seen as within the realm of educational psychology. In 1986, the construct of intelligence has become of interest in and of itself, apart from issues of prediction. The field of intelligence theory and research, as viewed by the experts in the field, seems to have broadened, to have become more mainstream with respect to psychology as a whole, and to have left behind the question of prediction as the driving force for understanding intelligence.

Frequencies of Listed Attributes

Table 1 lists 27 attributes that appeared in the present and past definitions of intelligence, and their frequencies in each of the two symposia. The small number of listings for each attribute would render formal statistical analysis hazardous. But some generalizations can nevertheless be made.

First, at least some general agreement exists across the two symposia regarding the nature of intelligence. The correlation between the two sets of frequencies is .50, indicating moderate overlap in present and past conceptions. Attributes such as adaptation to the environment, basic mental processes, and higher-order thinking (e.g., reasoning, problem solving, decision making) were prominent in both listings.

Second, certain themes recur in both symposia. The issue of the one versus the many—is intelligence one thing or is it manifold—continues to be of concern, although no consensus exists upon this matter. The issue of breadth of definition also continues to be of concern. As in the earlier symposium, some panelists define intelligence quite narrowly in terms of biological or especially cognitive elements, whereas others include a broader array of elements, including motivation and personality. The issue of breadth, like that of the one versus the many, remains unresolved. Investigators still disagree as to the relative emphases that should be placed in theory and research upon physiological versus behavioral manifestations of intel-

Table 1.   Frequencies of Attributes That Contributors Used to Define
Intelligence in 1986 and 1921

		1986		1921	
		No.	%	No.	%
1.	Adaptation, in order to meet the demands of the environment effectively	3	13	4	29
2.	Elementary processes (perception, sensation, attention)	5	21	3	21
3.	Metacognition (knowledge about cognition)	4	17	1	7
4.	Executive processes	6	25	1	7
5.	Interaction of processes and knowledge	4	17	0	0
6.	Higher-level components (abstract reasoning, representation, problem solving, decision making)	12	50	8	57
7.	Knowledge	5	21	1	7
8.	Ability to learn	4	17	4	29
9.	Physiological mechanisms	2	8	4	29
10.	Discrete set of abilities (e.g., spatial, verbal, auditory)	4	17	1	7
11.	Speed of mental processing	3	13	2	14
12.	Automated performance	3	13	0	0
13.	g	4	17	2	14
14.	Real-world manifestations (social, practical, tacit)	2	8	0	0
15.	That which is valued by culture	7	29	0	0
16.	Not easily definable, not one construct	4	17	2	14
17.	A field of scholarship	1	4	0	0
18.	Capacities prewired at birth	3	13	1	7
19.	Emotional, motivational constructs	1	4	1	7
20.	Restricted to academic/cognitive abilities	2	8	2	14
21.	Individual differences in mental competence	1	4	0	0
22.	Generation of environment based on genetic programming	1	4	0	0
23.	Ability to deal with novelty	1	4	1	7
24.	Mental playfulness	1	4	0	0
25.	Only important in its predictive value	0	0	1	7
26.	Inhibitive capacity	0	0	1	7
27.	Overt behavioral manifestations (effective/successful responses)	5	21	3	21

ligence, and the respective roles of process and product in defining intelligence also remain unresolved.

Third, despite the similarities in views over the 65 years, some salient
differences in the two listings can also be found. Metacognition—conceived
of as both knowledge about and control of cognition—plays a prominent
role in the 1986 symposium, but virtually no role at all in the 1921 symposium. The salience of metacognition and executive processes can undoubtedly be attributed to the predominance of the computer metaphor in
the current study of cognition and in information-processing approaches to
intelligence. In the present symposium, a greater emphasis has been placed
on the role of knowledge and the interaction between this knowledge and
mental processes. The change in emphasis is not entirely with respect to

Table 2. Behaviors Mentioned by Contributors for Definition of Intelligence

1986 Symposium	1921 Symposium
Anastasi 1 5 14 15 16	Buckingham 3 13 16 27
Baltes 16 17	Colvin 1 8
Baron 3 6 18 27	Dearborn 8
Berry 1 16	Freeman 2 4 6 11
Brown & Campione 3 4 8	Haggerty 2 6 16 18 20
Butterfield 3 4 6 7 8	Henmon 7 8 9
Carroll 6 10 11 13 14 15 20 27	Peterson 1 6 9 10
Das 2 4 6	Pintner 1 9 11 20 23
Detterman 2 10 13	Pressey 13 25
Estes 2 4 5	Ruml 2 6
Eysenck 2 9 11 13	Terman 6
Gardner 6 10 15 27	Thorndike 6 27
Glaser 6 7 12 15 18	Thurstone 6 19 26 27
Goodnow 15	Woodrow 1 6 8 9
Horn 6 10 11 12 16	
Humphreys 5	
Hunt 2 6 9	
Jensen 13 20	
Pellegrino 4 5 15 27	

(*continued*)

159

Table 2.   Behaviors Mentioned by Contributors
(*continued*)

1986 Symposium	1921 Symposium
Scarr 18 22	
Schank 3 6 7	
Sternberg 1 6 12 15 23 27	
Snow 4 6 7 8 21 24	
Zigler 6 7 8 19	

functions that occur within the organism. The present panelists show considerable emphasis upon the role of context, and particularly of culture, in defining intelligence, whereas such emphasis was absent in the earlier symposium.

Table 2 lists the contributors to the two symposia, and the behaviors from the list in Table 1 mentioned by each.

Crucial Next Steps in Intelligence Research

Investigators in both symposia were asked to list crucial next steps for research on intelligence. Table 3 lists the next steps that were suggested in each of the symposia, and the frequencies with which each of these steps was listed. Consider the following generalizations.

First, contributors to both symposia agreed upon the importance of investigating the development of intelligence, abilities other than cognitive ones, intelligence as it applies to specific domains, and real-life manifestations of intelligence. Thus, some overlap in future research priorities across the two symposia exists.

Second, salient differences as well as similarities were expressed in the suggested crucial next steps. Contributors to the 1921 symposium were much more concerned with statistical issues regarding intercorrelations of various tests, partial correlations, standardization, validity, and so on, than were contributors to the present symposium. Moreover, the 1921 panelists showed greater concern with future investigations of higher-level mental processes than did panelists of the 1986 symposium. This concern may well have been in response to the earlier emphasis on lower-level intellectual functions, such as sensory, motor, and simple perceptual processes by J. M. Cattell and others (e.g., Cattell, 1890). That these concerns became less

Table 3.   Crucial Next Steps in Intelligence Research

	1986		1921	
	No.	%	No.	%
1. Development of intelligence	5	21	4	29
2. Environmental demands and how they interact with intelligence	4	17	0	0
3. Elementary processes individuals use to solve problems	5	21	1	7
4. Delimit scope of field of intelligence	1	4	0	0
5. Training and modifiability of intelligence	3	13	1	7
6. Investigation of abilities other than cognitive (character, emotion, motivation)	6	25	7	50
7. Intelligence in specific domains (music, art, chess)	5	21	5	36
8. Investigation of intelligence in special populations (gifted, mentally retarded)	1	4	1	7
9. Investigation of physiological mechanisms of intelligence	5	21	0	0
10. Better tests of g	2	8	1	7
11. Laypeople's conceptions of intelligence	1	4	0	0
12. Moratorium on creation of new tests	1	4	0	0
13. Building precise models of cognitive tasks	3	13	0	0
14. Evolution of g	1	4	0	0
15. Tests of group factors	2	8	0	0
16. Higher-level processes of intelligence	0	0	2	14
17. Construct specific tests for specific purposes	2	8	0	0
18. Compensatory mechanisms in intelligent functioning	1	4	0	0
19. Learning and intelligence tests of dynamic nature	1	4	1	7
20. Interaction of knowledge and processes	2	8	0	0
21. Profile of intellectual abilities for persons' strengths and weaknesses	2	8	0	0
22. Ethological lines of evidence for intelligence	1	4	0	0
23. Large number of subjects in testing	1	4	0	0
24. Real-life manifestations of intelligence	5	21	2	14
25. Processes and structures of intelligence	1	4	0	0
26. Must be multiply determined	1	4	0	0
27. Mental playfulness/creativity	1	4	0	0
28. Intercorrelations and partial correlations between tests of intelligence	0	0	6	42
30. Form of intelligence in adult population	0	0	1	7
31. Nonverbal test of intelligence	0	0	2	14
32. Infant scale	0	0	1	7
33. Standardization of the composition, form, and scoring of intelligence tests	0	0	10	71
34. Race differences in intelligence	0	0	1	7
35. Heritability versus environmental influences on intelligence	0	0	1	7
36. Inform teachers as to how to interpret intelligence tests	0	0	1	7
37. Qualitative study of test situation	0	0	1	7
38. More careful treatment of errors	0	0	1	7
39. Relative weights of different tests in measuring intelligence	0	0	1	7
40. Revision of a calculation of mental age	0	0	1	7
41. Rating techniques for teachers	0	0	1	7
42. Reliability and validity of measures should be determined	0	0	1	7

salient is understandable, in that these crucial next steps did, in fact, occur after the 1921 symposium, and hence might well be seen as less pressing today. (For a review of the history of mental testing see Anastasi, 1976; Carroll, 1982.) The present panelists showed greater concern than the earlier ones with the analysis of demands of one's environment and how it interacts with intelligence, with building precise models of cognitive tasks, and with understanding better the elementary processes that contribute toward intelligence. The difference in concerns perhaps reflects the greater psychometric orientation that predominated in 1921 versus the greater information-processing as well as contextual orientation that predominates in 1986. In addition, the present panelists acknowledged the need in future research to investigate the physiological mechanisms of intelligence, whereas this concern was not mentioned in 1921.

Conclusion

The field of intelligence has evolved from one that concentrated primarily upon psychometric issues in 1921 to one that concentrates primarily upon information processing, cultural context, and their interrelationships in 1986. Prediction of behavior now seems to be somewhat less important than the understanding of that behavior, which needs to precede prediction. On the one hand, few if any issues about the nature of intelligence have been truly resolved. On the other hand, investigators of intelligence seem to have come a rather long way toward understanding the cognitive and cultural bases for the test scores since 1921.

REFERENCES

Anastasi, A. (1976). *Psychological testing* (4th ed.). New York: Macmillan.
Berry, J.W., & Dasen, P.R. (1974). Introduction. In J.W. Berry and P.R. Dasen (Eds.), *Culture and cognition: Readings in cross-cultural psychology* (pp. 1–25). London: Methuen.
Carroll, J.B. (1982). The measurement of intelligence. In R.J. Sternberg (Ed.), *Handbook of human intelligence* (pp. 29–120). Cambridge, England: Cambridge University Press.
Cattell, J.M. (1890). Mental tests and measurements. *Mind, 15,* 373–381.
Goddard, H.H. (1919). *Psychology of the normal and subnormal.* New York: Dodd, Mead.
Hale, M. (1982). History of employment testing. In A.K. Wigdor & W.R. Garner (Eds.), *Ability testing: Uses, consequences, and controversies* (Part II, pp. 3–38). Washington, DC: National Academy Press.

27.

Qualitative Integration: The Last Word?

Douglas K. Detterman
Case Western Reserve University

Sixty-five years ago, the first symposium of this sort was held to attempt to define intelligence. The scientific study of intelligence was less than 50 years old and IQ tests had been used for less than 20 years. The present symposium has the advantage of 65 years of additional work. The scientific study of intelligence is nearly a century and a quarter old and IQ tests have been in use for nearly 85 years. Further, testing permeates every major institution of our culture to an extent that would surely amaze even the most optimistic of the 1921 participants.

What should we expect to have come from this second symposium? How should we interpret this symposium in relation to the first one? Are there any signs of progress? Has intelligence been defined once and for all? Will another symposium be necessary 65 years from now?

Perhaps one of the most interesting findings from the quantitative analyses reported here by Sternberg and Berg is that the frequencies of major ideas mentioned in the two symposia correlate .50, about the same that IQ correlates with school grades. Some will interpret this correlation as an indication that not much has changed in 65 years, while others will regard it as an indication of the continuity of science. I think it indicates continuity.

An appropriate analogy might be to regard these two symposia as reports from explorers of a geographically complex frontier. The first symposium provided rough maps of the terrain specifying the most salient landmarks. The second symposium added detail to these basic charts.

Indeed, a most obvious difference between the first symposium and this one is that in this one the definitions are more elaborated. They include

163

more detail about what intelligence is and what it is not. The definitions in this symposium are more intricate.

Though the definitions provided by this symposium may be more refined, substantial disagreement on a single definition still abounds. It is probably foolish to expect this symposium, or even one held 65 years from now, to come to a unanimous conclusion. A concept as complex as intelligence probably cannot be captured by a single definition without gross oversimplification.

Bertrand Russell's advice to laymen on the interpretation of science seems appropriately applied here. His advice was that if the experts disagreed, the layman should withhold judgment, but if experts were in perfect agreement, then the layman could be sure that the opposite of what they agreed upon was true. It would be incorrect to interpret the disagreement apparent in this symposium as a sign that nobody knows what he or she is talking about. Rather, it would seem to me to be a sign of a healthy, vigorous scientific enterprise still in its formative stages.

It might be possible to attribute the diversity of opinion in this symposium to the wide range of participant interests. But that intelligence is no longer the exclusive realm of educational psychologists is an indication of the increasing vitality of the area. Researchers are realizing more fully the importance of understanding individual differences in mental ability as a key part of a fully developed theory of behavior. The study of human intelligence is becoming a respectable academic pursuit.

There were a number of issues raised in this symposium that were also raised in the 1921 symposium. Some of these issues can and should be settled before the next symposium, but others are not the kind of issues that can be resolved and will probably remain foci of interest as long as intelligence is studied. These issues deserve underlining.

Perhaps the most pervasive issue, and the one having the longest history, is the question of whether intelligence is a single thing or multiple things. Each position is adequately represented in this symposium, as it was in the first. Is g an adequate model of intellectual functioning as Spearman suggested, or are more elaborated models necessary to capture the full variety of individual differences? This question has extremely important implications not only for the study of intelligence but for the neuro- and behavioral sciences in general. My prediction is that the next decade will see an explosion of theoretical efforts on this question that will be unmatched even by the first two decades of this century, when the original work concerning g and its alternatives was conducted.

A number of secondary issues will be related to this major theoretical debate. One issue of concern will be the degree to which higher mental processes are causative or derivative of differences in intellectual abilities. One line of current thought suggests that metacognition, executive processes, or processes such as reasoning, problem solving, and decision making are primary causes of differences in intelligence. The opposing argument is that differences in these processes are derivative. They result because of differences in much more basic processes upon which these higher processes depend.

An issue that is likely to be of continuing concern is how intelligence develops. This question is of immense theoretical and practical concern. And though this may be the area in which the greatest advance has been made since the first symposium, it seems to me unlikely that many of the issues involved will be quickly resolved. For example, determining which aspects of environment are most important for the development of intelligence is an extremely complicated question that will certainly not be resolved overnight. I believe the study of intellectual development will proceed at a steady pace and will not be characterized by the lurches and theoretical explosions that might occur in other parts of the field.

There are a number of differences between the approaches of the 1921 and 1986 symposia. Perhaps the most important of these is that the study of intelligence has now been placed in a much broader social context. Throughout this symposium there is concern for the societal and cross-cultural implications that models of intellectual functioning may have. Part of this attention was certainly the result of the turbulent history of intelligence testing over the last twenty-five years. But it would be a mistake to attribute all of the interest in this topic to social turbulence.

Intelligence is a socially important attribute of individuals and, for better or worse, the perception of this attribute has major consequences for the treatment of people by their society. There is growing interest in understanding the social importance of intelligence, not only because of its impact on social policy but also because it is theoretically important to do so. Any fully developed theory of intelligence will have to specify the interaction of intelligence with social context.

Another new development in this symposium is the interest in "real-world" intelligence. We have discovered that intelligence may be displayed in places other than the classroom. Though it is possible that instances of intelligence have been so rare in the real world as to escape notice, there are probably better explanations for this recent interest. More likely is the growing assumption that what explains academic performance may not be the same thing that explains important behaviors outside the classroom.

For this comparison and the contrast of the 1921 symposium with the present one, I have used only a few of the most salient examples. They are no more than examples. To appreciate fully the similarities and differences, both symposia must be read. After doing that, I believe two conclusions are obvious: (a) A good deal of progress has been made in conceptualizing intelligence, this most complicated and important construct; (b) there is an enormous amount of work that needs to be done.

For those who expected to read this volume and obtain the definitive definition of intelligence, I apologize. It is unlikely that any symposium of this sort ever will provide the last word. But good theory and research based on such a symposium will. When a definitive definition is developed, there will be no need for symposia of this sort. Until then, they will help to describe what has been discovered and suggest what can be hoped for in the future.

Author Index

Subject Index